"Whether Joel Schalit is v
Zionism, or punk rock, *Je*
from the battle front. The rage of the disillusioned true believer cries throughout these pages and gives them an edge of harsh immediacy that is notably absent in most developed radical thought. Implicit in Schalit's work is the notion that the ongoing growth of religious fundamentalism poses a unique challenge to left-wing intellectuals and organizers. In place of analysis, Schalit continuously insists, many progressives seem to believe that by endlessly repeating easy assessments of the enemy that the benighted foot soldiers of spiritual intolerance will see the light and disperse. Ironically, however, the very existence of the religious right in America is an indictment of the left's limited mass appeal. So, is the American left eternally consigned to a cycle of impotence? Not if Schalit has anything to say about it. In some of his boldest passages, he insists that a critical recovery of the vast reservoir of ideas of the historical left, especially those of European progressivism, ought to be recalled in much the same way that conservatives continually bring to bear their faith in God and market to a profane present incapable of redemption.

"Schalit's perspective is largely a product of a frightfully schizophrenic childhood, raised by a Holocaust-generation, globe-trotting multilingual widower for whom politics and family life were inseparable. A scion of a founding labor Zionist family from Latvia who first settled in Palestine in 1882, Schalit acquired his initial political insights alongside of an encyclopedic knowledge of modern armaments in a highly militarized country. In one of *Jerusalem Calling's* most poignant passages, Schalit underscores the difference between dream and reality when he describes his visit to a collectively owned McDonald's franchise on an Israeli kibbutz. Nothing could better crystallize the kinds of first-person encounters with history's brutal contradictions than this unfortunate tribute to agrarian collectivism gone terribly wrong."

—David Grad, *New York Press*

JERUSALEM CALLING

A Homeless Conscience in a Post-Everything World

JOEL SCHALIT

Akashic Books
New York

Published by Akashic Books

Design, layout, and photography by Courtney Utt
Photograph on page 167 by David Schalit

ISBN: 1-888451-17-3
Library of Congress Card Number: 00-112240

First printing
Printed in Canada

Akashic Books
PO Box 1456
New York, NY 10009
Akashic7@aol.com
www.akashicbooks.com

Portions of *Jerusalem Calling* have appeared in earlier form in *Punk Planet*, the *San Francisco Bay Guardian*, the *Journal of Mundane Behavior*, and *Bad Subjects: Political Education for Everyday Life*.

For Abba, Naomi, and David
In Memory of Michael Aryeh (1953-2001)

ACKNOWLEDGMENTS

I'd like to thank Charlie Bertsch, this book's editor and my close pal of nearly a decade, for taking so much of his time to shepherd this text into a readable form. Charlie's ideas for piecing everything together were beautifully creative, as was the way in which he helped shape this book's language. Indeed, it was Charlie who suggested in 1995 that everything I had been working on since we'd first met was part of a larger text that would someday come into being. I can't thank Charlie enough for seeing it through to completion.

Of equal importance in this text's production has been my publisher and friend Johnny Temple. For his immense patience, wise editorial insights, and for the high expectations that he placed on this book, I am grateful beyond words. The shared cultural background Johnny brought to this project—punk rock and a love of good reggae—was crucial in assuring that my transition to making books was a logical continuation of the literary independence I've been blessed with all these years.

I'd like to thank Dan Sinker at *Punk Planet* and all my homeys at *Bad Subjects* for helping me become a writer—and for providing a consistently supportive environment in which it was possible to experiment without the constraints of academic writing or the law of the market. Hopefully, as time progresses, these two magazines will be recognized for their contributions to the intellectual excellence and boundless creativity of America's battered countercultures.

I can't express enough gratitude to my father Elie Schalit, who went out of his way to help me score permission to use the photograph on the cover of this book, "Soldiers at the Wall." This was also made possible through the assistance of journalist Eitan Haber and the Israel Government Press Office, who kindly put up with my persistent requests for a hard copy of the image.

I'd also like to extend a special shout-out to the professors and instructors who used the original *Bad Subjects* essays from which some of this book was derived in their course materials at Earlham College, Cornell University, the University of Utah, Bluffton College, and the Center for Popular Music Research at Berlin's Humboldt University. Thanks for taking my work so seriously; it has been incredibly encouraging.

Last but not least, I want to thank my non-literary sources of inspiration for sticking by me and keeping me alive: my big brother David, for showing me what it means to have integrity under the most difficult of life's circumstances; my longstanding collaborator and friend Vance Galloway, the only man I'd consider calling a "post-guitar player"; and to the lovely Courtney Utt, the outstanding photographer who designed this book and let me "court" her with the first chapters of this book.

Hamburg, Germany, 1999

CONTENTS

Preface	15
America the Enchanted	21
Seeing Red	87
Down and Out with Rock and Roll	125
My Own Private Israel	163
Epilogue	213

PREFACE

The title of this book came to me on a bleak winter day in Jerusalem last year. I had just walked through the Jaffa Gate into the Old City, when, amidst the din of vendors hawking fresh pita bread to American tourists and Israeli border police commanding merchants to keep their carts moving, I heard the sounds of electronic music emanating from an alleyway within the shouk. Something about the music was alluring, and as my companion and I moved toward the loud beats, we stumbled upon a tiny stall full of compact discs ranging from Egyptian diva Om Kholtum and the French Elvis Johnny Halliday to British avant-electroid Aphex Twin. To call this an example of Shimon Peres's "New Middle East" would be an understatement.

Trying to appear somewhat inconspicuous so as to avoid a mad sales pitch, I addressed the owner of the store in Hebrew. I picked up a copy of The Clash's *London Calling* and asked, *"Kama ze oleh?"* ("How much does this cost?")

"Arbaim veh tesha Shekel" ("Forty-nine Shekels"), the Palestinian merchant answered with disappointment, recognizing that I was not a tourist he could overcharge.

On the album cover, the legendary photograph of Paul Simonon smashing his bass guitar was somewhat blurry, and I immediately grew suspicious. I flipped the CD over and observed that the liner notes on the back tray were also obscured, particularly the Epic Records logo, which was missing the letter "c".

I laughed at the poor reproduction job but was nevertheless delighted to have stumbled upon it. After all, this was a bootleg of a recording by a band that trafficked in outlaw imagery and had even released an album called *Black Market Clash* (featuring the silhouette of a Rastafarian in a face-off with British riot police). "Maybe these guys should have called this bootleg *Jerusalem Calling,*" I joked, as I left the shop and moved further into the Old City.

The fact that something so typically British had been reconfigured by the local economy to appear so distinctly Middle Eastern left a very strong impression on me. In the final stages of editing this book, I decided to run an Internet search on the words "Jerusalem Calling." More than forty different uses of the phrase turned up, including various prophetic evangelical tracts and an MP3 of Jerry Sullivan and Tammy's song, "Hear Jerusalem Calling." I also discovered references to another book with the same title, written fifty-one years ago by Dutch journalist Pierre Van Paassen.

In a litigious culture in which the rights to intellectual property are hotly debated, this last discovery brought on a bit of anxiety. After making a few phone calls to ascertain the legal status of my situation, I immediately set out to acquire a copy of Van Paassen's book and gather biographical information about him. What I found not only allayed my concerns, but ultimately enriched the experience of putting together my own *Jerusalem Calling.*

A Dutch immigrant to the US, Van Paassen worked for various North American newspapers, such as the *New York Evening World*, in which he covered devil-worship services at Satanic masses in Paris, and Toronto's *Daily Star*, where he served as a correspondent during the Spanish Civil War, interviewing such legendary figures as the anarchist guerrilla Buenaventura Durutti. Van Paassen's interest in anti-capitalism and religious obscurantism stemmed from a sharp appraisal of the political and spiritual currents overtaking Europe before the Second World War, which included the revival of occultism that had developed in Nazi Germany and the strains of anarchism and communism in the battle against Franco in Spain. As *Jerusalem Calling*'s essays on the struggles of the religious and anarcho-socialist labor movements in post-war France and Italy demonstrate, Van Paassen also held a life-long fascination with the idea of a progressivism free from any alignment with either Stalinist Russia or Anglo-American imperialism. While traveling through Europe during the late 1940s, Van Paassen evaluated the possibilities for a more just and egalitarian society emerging from the havoc created by the war. In the chaos, he perceived opportunities for neo-Marxist redistribution of feudal land holdings and the establishment of a living wage system.

Van Paassen's positions do not seem that out of the ordinary for an educated European radical of his generation. Nor, for that matter, for a post–Cold War progressive today. What surprised me was his now-dated appreciation of the revolutionary example set by the establishment of the state of Israel. A classically Protestant philo-Semite, Van Paassen saw in the history of ancient Jerusalem the embryo of a socialist Athens in which the struggles of the Jewish people to live free from foreign domination, in the service of an anti-imperialist God, became the origins of the Enlightenment tradition of radical politics. The rise of a Jewish nation after two thousand years of exile was the *next* stage of God's plan, so that a just, spiritually savvy republic would emerge as an example for the rest of the anarchic post-war world to follow. Though Van Paassen was fixated on Israel, perhaps his ideas were more suited to Tito's Yugoslavia.

Given the developments in the Middle East over the past fifty years, Van Paassen's notions about Israel seem awkward, especially the positive slant he put on the nation's treatment of the local Arab population. As Edward Said, Benny Morris, and many other Palestinian and Israeli scholars have more than adequately demonstrated, the 700,000 or so Palestinians left homeless by the 1948 war did not exactly leave willingly. Both right-wing and left-wing Jewish military organizations encouraged their flight. Yet Van Paassen was so enamored by the progressive elements of Zionist political ideology, including its reconciliation of socialism with religion, that he uncritically bought into what Hebrew University political scientest Ze'ev Sternhell labels "the founding myths of Israel." Like many progressives of his generation, Van Paassen clearly had his blind spots. Particularly revealing is how he became involved with the Irgun Zvai Lehumi ("National Military Organization"), best known for its role in the ethnic cleansing of the Arab village of Deir Yassin in 1948—and for its ultra-nationalist politics.

Having unknowingly written a book with the same title as Van Paassen's, I began to feel that his words were a long-delayed reply from the other side of the post-revolutionary fence. While I can't claim to be a red-diaper baby, I am the youngest child in a family of three generations whose members' lives have been indelibly shaped by the very struggle for national self-realization in Israel that Van Paassen's book places so much hope in. Indeed, the only disciplined political organization that I've ever belonged to has been my own family. Consequently, I've grown up with a worldview largely structured around political ideology. While reading Van Paassen's religiously inspired pages, I could not help but think that our shared history was some kind of fabrication that should never have incorporated the notion of collective emancipation—least of all, mine. It is as if we have all been acting out roles in someone else's fetishization of us as a chosen people, rather than following our own script and determining our own self-worth.

Jews have never been anyone's *chosen* anything. Yet history has certainly marked us, and we definitely have our "crosses" to bear. As much as I would like to believe that the Jewish struggle for self-determination has always brought out the best in us, the current crisis besetting Israel attests that we could have done a lot better. Yes, there are outstanding achievements that we have made as a people, especially in terms of cultivating successive classes of radical intellectuals and social critics; I want to hold onto these now more than ever. But, to paraphrase Karl Marx, another Jewish product of the Enlightenment, when it came to fashioning a country, we did so under conditions that were not of our own choosing.

Joel Schalit
San Francisco, October 2001

Courtney's house, San Diego, California, 1999

AMERICA THE ENCHANTED

When I was fifteen, my older sister Naomi enrolled me in an Episcopal boarding school in Portland, Oregon. I was already a seasoned world traveler: I had spent many hours hanging out in Italian roadside cafés, experienced the excitement of a London turned upside down by the first wave of punk, and had wandered the streets of New York's Lower East Side with friends looking for a fix, whether from music or drugs. Yet Portland opened my eyes. To be sure, the city was cultivating a sophisticated air with its used bookstores, early punk bands, and coffee houses. But the Portland I got to know during the Reagan era was different from the Portland of today. Underneath the shiny façade of urban renewal was a place where the WASP provincialism and prejudice of middle-America still ruled with an iron hand. For a cosmopolitan boy from nowhere, the experience was staggering.

My first emotional response to life in my new home was an overwhelming depression. Maybe it was the perpetually bad weather. Maybe it was because everyone I met was so terribly nice and well-mannered. But the immense silence that pervaded every mandatory Wednesday chapel service was a far cry from the shouting and frenzy of my family's Mediterranean world. The way the ministers spoke down to students when they read comic books instead of Bibles was the antithesis of the Jewish culture I had grown up in.

For the first time, I began to think of religion as an objective structure separate from everyday life. Other students seemed to confront their own religion as an institution to rebel against. I couldn't understand that. In Israel, the feeling was altogether different, as it must have been for many American Jews. You were Jewish whether you liked it or not. You didn't have to go to synagogue; Judaism was inescapable because it was in your blood. And after attending chapel once a week for a short period at Oregon Episcopal School, I began to realize that I was in a religious community whose sense of cultural identity was maintained by practices far more complex than simply attending mandatory worship services.

I remember storming out of a lecture by the chaplain of Andover-Newton when I was a sophomore. He was giving us the only seminar in sex education I would ever receive in high school. He had started to tell us that since it would be practically impossible for him to prevent us from having premarital sex, we should, at the very least, invite Christ into our sexual activities as an active, third partner. Enraged, I stood up in front of the entire student body and told the minister off.

"Do you realize that you don't have a captive audience?" I yelled. "I happen to be a Jew, and I can tell you that there also happen to be Muslims, Hindus, and an animist from Thailand here, too!" As I left the chapel, my classmates looked up at me in total disbelief. One female student immediately apologized on behalf of the entire student body for my rude and offensive outburst. My punishment? I was confined to the dorms for the weekend without my weekly allowance of ten dollars.

I wasn't always so ornery. If anything, I endeavored to be a model student because I felt so unequal to my classmates: I didn't have any of my own money, my sneakers always had holes in them, and my jeans were perpetually torn. Where I thought I could prevail was in my religion classes and in my devotion to the one physical activity I knew none of the jocks had any patience for—mountaineering. It was in the climbing program that I met Father Doctor Thomas Goman, a high school teacher with a doctorate in theology from Harvard Divinity School, who was purported to have been the head of the Students for a Democratic Society in Cambridge at one point in his life.

Rumor had it that Tom had blown up a Selective Service administration building in Boston to protest American involvement in Vietnam. But Tom had gotten all of that out of his system by the time he came to our school. Nevertheless, his legend preceded him to the point that many of us mistook his radical past for his prep-school present. Students revered him as though he were a prophet. And I was pretty impressed with him myself. Most of all, Tom was a great philosophy teacher. We read Herman Hesse novels together, discussed Camus and Sartre, and spoke about Zen during our many weekends climbing Mount Hood and hiking through the Oregon desert.

Tom was becoming a second father to me. As I got to know him better, though, I began to sense that he was troubled. At the end of my junior year, I got a job working for the Forest Service in Crater Lake. I had a couple of weeks off before my seasonal contract began so Tom invited me to stay with his family in southeast Portland. I had a lot of fun at first, listening to his old Fugs records, reading his dissertation on the concept of human sacrifice in Nietzsche and the Vedas. It never dawned on me what these records and writings said about Tom and where his life would take him. All I really noticed was how they contributed to my idealized conception of him as a perfect mix of rock and roll, politics, and a sustained commitment to thinking. Besides, it was of utmost importance for me to meet educated adults who were still true to their sixties past. This was the only remedy I had for all the Docksiders, Polo shirts, and piety that flooded my high school. In retrospect, what was so dangerous about my circumstance was that my need to overcome a superficial sense of stifling conservatism expressed itself in a desire to take on the identities of my teachers. I didn't understand how the new political landscape of the Reagan era had thrown these very people into crisis. Tom was perhaps the most extreme example. Whenever a teacher would organize students to participate in a demonstration—such as sitting on train tracks to bar the government from transporting MX missiles through Oregon—Tom never showed up. When I would ask him why he didn't attend any of these events, he would always reply that there was simply nothing he could do anymore.

Despite my overwhelming naïveté, it gradually became clear to me that Tom had directed his efforts elsewhere. In his ethics class, he reveled in Kant, Mill, and Plato; in his geometry class, his enthusiasm was even more pronounced in his almost spiritual passion for trigonometry and proofs. But math was one place where I couldn't go along for the ride. I was dyslexic, I'd never been able to get anything above a D in Algebra, and I consistently failed to complete even the most basic assignments. This was where Tom and I began to part ways.

I confronted him one day in his office before going home to San Francisco for Christmas vacation. "Tom, I really can't do this work and it galls me. Why can't you acknowledge that and just recognize that I am indeed trying?"

Tom took off his glasses, sat down, and stared blankly out the window. "Look, Joel," he said in a tired and exasperated voice, "you're a great mountain climber, you write beautifully, and you've learned how to think these last three years. There's no reason why a boy like you cannot do equations when the world you live in is built on the math you claim not to understand."

Peering down to avoid seeing the expression on his face, I responded, "Maybe so, but I can't see why you have so much invested in proving that to me when I'm never going to have to study this shit again."

Aroused, Tom finally turned away from the window, looked me in the eye, and said the most outrageous thing I had ever heard: "Because math is the expression of God's mind in the world. By now, I was hoping you would have figured this out and learned why you should come to Jesus Christ. Obviously you haven't, and I have only myself to blame for that." It was the first and last time we ever spoke directly about Christianity.

I spent the rest of the school year failing Tom's class. Yet I continued training with him and the mountaineering team to take the sophomores up Mount Hood in May for the annual climb. During our downtime, I'd sit in my room depressed, listening over and over to Hüsker Dü, trying to meditate in order to achieve some sense of the holiness Tom had found lacking in me. But it never really went anywhere. Bob Mould's furious, mantra-like yelling of "New Day Rising" was more cathartic than the asthmatic breathing techniques I was learning from my Alan Watts books. My attempts at becoming more spiritual earned the respect of my peers who were discovering Jack Kerouac and the Grateful Dead; I, however, still needed Tom's approval.

By the middle of my senior year in 1986, I had managed to get over the culture shock of being one of the only Jews in the school. Turning to Buddhism, however superficially, I had found a way to participate in the religious culture of the institution without necessarily buying into the religion of my friends and teachers. Buddhism was instrumental in putting a critical distance between Tom and me because it helped me overcome the sense of rejection that the entire community instilled in me. It was somehow related to nature. In *Introduction to Zen*, D.T. Suzuki argued that Christianity is based on the belief that man is supposed to dominate nature. As simpleminded as Suzuki's pronouncement was, it had a remarkable effect on me. The only remaining positive aspect of my relationship with Tom was the mountaineering program. For the first time, I was able to discern the religious origins of Tom's need to climb mountains. And start criticizing them, too.

The two practice climbs we performed prior to the annual sophomore outing took place in January and April. During the first training session, we performed a harrowing winter ascent of Mount Hood. After running out of mantras to take my mind off of the altitude sickness, I was saved by Tom's request to escort one of our team members down the Hog's Back, four thousand feet to the lodge. She had become sick and it would have been unwise at that angle to let her go down alone. Besides, I wanted to get back to the comfort of Timberline Lodge with its coffee machines, magazines, and overweight Saint Bernards sitting beneath piles of snow next to the hotel entrance.

But something was still bothering me. The weather had grown positively awful. It was almost midday, we'd been climbing since two in the morning, and Tom had a snowy and cold 1,500 feet of climbing left. "Make sure to turn around in an hour if you haven't made much more progress!" I yelled out to him in the howling wind.

"You bet, Joel!" he replied, as he fastened his climbing harness and began the last stage of the ascent with his two remaining students. His severe determination to soldier on reminded me of the chapter of the Bible we'd just read in religion class in which Moses climbs Mount Sinai to receive the Ten Commandments.

Three hours passed before I began to get nervous. It was four o'clock and there was no sign of them on the Palmer snowfield. Binoculars were of no use because the snow was falling fairly heavily and the Hog's Back was covered in clouds. My neighbor Eric, who had come down at the very beginning of the climb, said that he wasn't too concerned. But it was getting dark and it wasn't like Tom to take such risks by staying out so late. He'd been on the mountain for over fourteen hours, risking the avalanche hazards of climbing during the day, and the weather was closing in. Slightly reassured by Eric, I retired to the day lodge after deciding I'd put a call through to mountain rescue if Tom hadn't arrived by sunset; I knew he didn't have any lighting equipment or flashlights with him and had, as usual, left his sleeping bag with me.

At five, I made the decision to take a final look outside before darkness eliminated the remnants of visibility not already obscured by the snow. As I walked out of the lodge, Tom emerged from a snow bank with his two companions and fell to the pavement. I picked him up, berating him for having endangered himself, not to mention the safety and welfare of the two students. Tom remained silent. When he removed his hood, I noticed his face had turned a deep purple, and his balance was unsteady. Taking off his iced-over glasses, Tom declared that his kidneys had started bleeding again. Astounded by this revelation, I was left speechless. The subject never arose again and I repressed all thoughts about it. I did not want to acknowledge the risks he had incurred by having remained on the mountain for so long in such bad physical condition.

Everything else Tom revealed to me that year chipped away at his omnipotence. Though I kept trying to conform to his desire for me to get closer to God, I simply couldn't; and it was clear to both of us that my flirtation with Buddhism was merely a passing fad. Even as Tom's authority began to lose its weight, he would still express occasional dismay over the failings of my spiritual efforts. "All that Zen and existentialism won't get you anywhere," he stated, as we got into his car for our second and last training session on a rock towering over the Sandy River near the Columbia Gorge. "It's empty. At the very least, it ought to teach you that the mental discipline meditation requires is the same discipline you should be applying to trigonometry."

As we unloaded the ropes and the carabiners from the back of his car, it dawned on me how symbolic my Buddhism was in light of what Tom had said. This was the only spiritual practice I could embrace in order to prevent myself from losing my own sense of Jewishness. If I were to give in to the equally superficial option of replacing meditation with the practice of mathematics, I would, in a sense, be converting to Christianity. Feeling a little uneasy, I bound myself with ropes as though I were a Hasid in front of the Wailing Wall, and began the ascent of the precipice off of which we planned to rappel in preparation for the annual twelfth-grade wilderness trip at the end of the school year.

Once we reached the summit, our instructions were to anchor a rappelling line to a tree. Then we were supposed to practice belaying, lowering our partners slowly to prevent them from falling. We were all visibly nervous. To make it clear what kinds of hazards were at stake, Tom volunteered to be the first member of our group to rappel off the face of the rock. As my friend Mike settled into his harness, we anchored his waist on a safety line that we had attached to a tree. We had to allow for some slack in Mike's own safety line because if Tom fell rather quickly, Mike's hip would break. When our preparations were finished, Tom took off his helmet, screamed "On belay?" and took a swan dive off of the cliff—before Mike had the chance to reply "Belay on!"

Looking out over the ledge, I could see Tom's body bang sharply against the jagged walls of the cliff. When we noticed Mike rapidly sliding toward the edge, unable to hold onto Tom, we ran to his rescue to prevent the rope from sliding any further. Tom's fall broke before he killed himself. In silence, we cautiously lowered him to the bottom. This routine was repeated eight more times. By the end of it, Tom was covered in blood, his dry, frail skin punctured extensively by rocks. We were all extremely shaken. For the first time in nearly four months, I thought about his kidneys. When we arrived at our cars, I asked Tom whether he was going to go to the hospital. As he put on his favorite denim shirt, the one with a record of his most ambitious climbs stitched onto it, the blood from his wounds obscured the names of the peaks he'd bagged over the course of his life. "Oh no, I'll just bandage them myself when I get home," he replied.

By the time we returned to campus, I was so incensed by the whole affair that I spoke to the rest of the climbing team about bringing the matter up with the director of the school's outdoor program. Much to my chagrin, no one volunteered. I went ahead and spoke to the director anyway. After describing the day's events, I said, "I know this sounds ridiculous, but it struck me as something like a perverted act of penitence to prove his own faith." The director found this too hard to take and threw me out of his office. To this day, I take no pleasure in having been correct in my interpretation of Tom's actions. But I hope that the director never, ever forgets how wrong he was not to have taken my fears seriously.

On May 9, Tom called me into his office to tell me that he did not want me to accompany him on the first sophomore climb of the season. "There are fifty tenth-graders this year," he said. "And you've got a geometry exam the day after the climb. If you don't pass it, you're not going to graduate from high school. Take the weekend to study for it and go up with the second and third groups later. I'll find a replacement for you." Saddened that I was not going to be able to go up with him one last time before I graduated, I resigned myself to staying home.

The day before the climb, I listened to the radio as I tried in vain to solve practice equations. Toward the end of the evening edition of "All Things Considered," Oregon Public Broadcasting announced that a storm warning was in effect for the Cascade Mountain region. I got on the phone and called Tom to tell him. "Don't worry," he said reassuringly. "I already checked with the Forest Service. We'll suspend the climb as soon as it becomes apparent that a storm is about to hit."

At two o'clock on Sunday morning, Tom began the ascent of Mount Hood with eighteen students and faculty in tow. Several members of the group defected early on due to altitude sickness. By four the next afternoon, the worst storm in Mount Hood's recorded history had kicked in. Thirteen members of the climbing party remained on the mountain, stranded at ten thousand feet. There are several different accounts of what transpired after that. The most consistent one contends that the snow had reduced visibility to zero, so Tom was forced to set a compass bearing to guide the party back down. But it was set sixty degrees off and the group ended up on the southeastern side of the mountain amidst a series of glaciers and deep crevasses.

When it became clear that he had made a serious error, Tom ordered everyone to build a snow-cave to sit out the storm. For some reason, he had everyone jettison their stoves, food, and sleeping bags to better fit into the cave. The next day, the two most experienced climbers slid down the mountain on their backpacks to warn the authorities about what had happened. Unfortunately, the rescue effort could not be convened until Thursday the 16th, when the weather finally cleared.

I spent that day acting as the student representative for the school's outdoor program. As I stood in front of the chapel, reporters peppered me with questions, praising my skills as a mountaineer to try to prod details out of me. "C'mon, Joel," a CBS Evening News reporter said. "Is this guy Goman a lunatic or what? You were his chief assistant, you should know."

"Listen," I responded, as several reporters flocked around me, "the question of culpability isn't even an issue yet. Nature is indiscriminate, and when you engage in activities such as mountain climbing, sometimes things are out of your control." For all the quasi-Buddhist wisdom of the statement, I knew I might be wrong.

At four that afternoon, the school announced that a snow-cave full of bodies had finally been found. Our new chaplain grabbed me and said that we were going to Emmanuel Hospital, where National Guard helicopters were flying victims in a desperate attempt to save them. We waited around for several hours while doctors heated up the climbers' frozen bodies, hoping to revive them. Midway through the evening, a physician's representative announced that the chances of survival were slim because the average core temperature was fifty degrees below zero.

Before deaths began to be officially announced, we were brought several pieces of clothing in order to identify the victims. "Their bodies are too bloated to facilitate proper recognition," I was told. "So we thought that since you trained these kids, you might have an idea what they were wearing."

I recalled what I could. "Yes, that's it; that's Tasha Amy's jacket," I said, pointing out the last piece of clothing I could identify. By that point I was too overcome with anger to be of much help to anyone. Tasha was the one student in the program I had strongly objected to being allowed to participate in the climb. She was eighty-percent blind, but Tom had overruled me, saying that she would be the first to be sent down to the lodge under any sign of danger. As usual, no one had listened to me, and a fifteen-year-old girl was dead as a result.

When I got home, I found the dorms unlocked and students wandering listlessly around the parking lot. None of the deaths had been announced by the hospital yet. Everyone wanted to know who had died. All I could do was tell them that I didn't know. The air surrounding the school was remarkable. All the regulations and solemnity had been suspended by the crisis. Students were smoking in the television room, one of the resident advisors was openly drunk, and televisions were broadcasting the latest news about the accident—from everywhere, it seemed. Staring at one of the sets, I saw Tom's frozen body being carted off the rear-loading ramp of an army helicopter. At that moment, I remembered how Abraham had been required to prove his faith to God by demonstrating that he was willing to sacrifice his son, Isaac. But in the end, Abraham never actually had to take his son's life, or his own.

All of a sudden, it felt like the religious proselytizing I had endured for three and a half years had finally clicked. Not only had these gentiles taught this homeless Jew his scripture, I thought, they had also taught me a lesson about faith—theirs *and* mine. "Some education," I muttered to myself, as I wandered off into the darkness to cry.

My years in the Portland boarding school really did prove to be "some education." But it wasn't due to my classes so much as to my exposure to Protestantism, American-style. On the surface, it might seem like there was little to connect the extreme behavior of one disillusioned teacher with a school that prides itself on being a model of well-heeled liberal tolerance. I'm sure that's the story the school's lawyers would sell you. In the aftermath of the Mount Hood disaster, however, I had come to see how easily a façade of open-minded rationality could conceal darker motives. In the end, the powers-that-be at my school were only slightly less zealous in their desire to convert me than their far more extreme counterparts would have been at Four Square Church in conservative Springfield, Oregon. I was a Jew. And as a Jew, I was a historical anachronism. The challenge, therefore, was to rescue me from my religion by any means necessary, even math.

Facing up to the fallout of my parochial-school education has not been easy. The most difficult aspect is dealing with people's confusion over my intense preoccupation with religion. In the minds of certain progressives I've encountered over the years, my interests are symptomatic of a regressive sentimentality that betrays my bourgeois origins. I might be flirting with the radical chic, but I'm never going to stop being a pseudo-revolutionary poseur. In the hearts of many a religious person I've met, my preoccupations suggest a dark night of the soul that I'll undoubtedly overcome when I line my psyche up with the right archetype, be it Jesus, a good relationship, the right therapist, or somewhere else the divine might shine. I can see why they're suspicious. I have two degrees in religious studies. I spent years making fun of evangelical Christians—particularly Christian talk radio—in an audio collage group called the Christal Methodists. I'm writing my doctoral dissertation on the role of religion in Marxist critical theory, and I have written many articles on various other aspects of religion. At one point in my life, I would have felt no need to justify my interest in religion. But now that I'm older and more patient, I do try to explain.

Unfortunately, this usually doesn't work too well. Religion is one of those subjects people simply aren't prepared to talk about. I'm forever annoyed by individuals who assume that my preoccupation is in some way pathological, as if adopting a critical stance toward religion were a tell-tale sign of madness. I obviously do have deeply personal reasons for thinking about religion. Significant events in my life have convinced me in a visceral way of religion's importance. The Mount Hood disaster is but one example. As my high school years in Portland demonstrated all too clearly, when you're a wandering Jew like myself, you can't pretend that religion doesn't matter. That's why my analyses of American fundamentalism and radical sects are no less personal for me than the firsthand experiences of which I write. I have come to see how religion—and popular music, for that matter, as I will discuss later in this book—can highlight how the experiences of an individual are much more than individual experiences. Yes, I care about religion. But so should you, no matter how different your life may be from my own. And if you're an American, the reasons for caring are doubly powerful.

In the very final stage of editing this book, the Twin Towers of the World Trade Center in New York City were destroyed in a tragic terrorist attack that took the lives of thousands of innocent people. Although the smoke has not yet cleared as of this writing, it seems likely that religious fundamentalism played a central role. While my discussion here focuses primarily on the frightening faces of Jewish and Christian fundamentalism, my admonitions can clearly be directed at fundamentalism of any stripe. One of the most common responses that I heard in the aftermath of this horrific disaster was, "God bless America." Though dismayed by the prevalence of this sentiment—one that seems to say, "Ours is the *real* God"—I can't say that I was surprised.

If there is such a thing as a singular "American ideology," it is reflected in the way Americans think about religion. Americans are a people notoriously unconcerned with the nuances of philosophy, but just as notoriously obsessed with religious issues. Even questions of secular philosophy are usually filtered through a religious framework. To be sure, this filtering is often unconscious. But this only makes it more powerful. When Americans are distancing themselves from religion, they still do so in religious terms. The motto "In God We Trust" on the dollar bill of the first secular state of modern times is no anomaly. (For that matter, nor is the Bush administration's employment of words like "crusade," and the Department of Defense's brief use of the term "infinite justice" to describe their war against terrorism.) When we consider religion in the United States, however, we are confronted with a field of intense contestation. The battles between the United States' innumerable sects are the backdrop for a more basic conflict.

In discussing the role of religion in public life, there are two dominant and competing points of view. The "American ideology," in fact, delimits not a unified body of concepts, but the no-man's-land that divides the two warring perspectives. American liberals have traditionally regarded religion as a private affair concerned only with the health, stability, and well-being of the individual. This is the perspective that informs the foundational documents of the American nation, including the transcendentalist writings of Ralph Waldo Emerson and Henry David Thoreau, and William James's highly influential turn-of-the-century treatise, *The Varieties of Religious Experience*, in which he self-consciously brackets all considerations of community and politics to get at the supposed "essence" of religious feeling. To return to the example of the Mount Hood disaster, this liberal perspective would attribute Father Tom Goman's extremism to his personal understanding—or misunderstanding—of the Word, not to any broader social context.

This liberal perspective contrasts sharply with the example set by the Commonwealth of Massachusetts. Far more concerned with the *politics* of religion, the Commonwealth was a theocracy before it became a secular unit of the United States. Throughout US history, religious minorities have advocated abolishing the separation of church and state in the same theocratic spirit. Although the liberal perspective on religion has remained hegemonic, over time this theocratic perspective has put enough pressure on the state to give American life a religious aura that sometimes disturbs people from other industrialized countries—even from countries with official religions. Whenever periods of religious decline have made it seem that complete secularization was imminent, new religious movements have sprung up to ward it off.

What is unique about American ideology is that it fosters the illusion that America was the first country to have been liberated from the tyranny of tradition. The nation's "Founding Fathers" imagined a republic of inherently democratic, egalitarian individuals capable of following Kant's axiom that men must become their own legislators. The constitutional separation of church and state has done a great deal to promote this belief. This is not lost on the religious right, which has tried to expose America's liberal ideologies of religious tolerance and freedom of conscience to be smoke screens concealing sectarian agendas. The hazards of this reasoning become obvious when we examine the solutions that the religious right advocates imposing on the American polity.

For the most part, the religious right has successfully disguised its own agenda by expressing its critique with terms borrowed from the language of multiculturalism and civil rights: By prohibiting prayer in public schools, the state *discriminates* against the right of the religious majority to express their own freedom of conscience; by tolerating the murder of unborn children, the government selectively abrogates its obligation to protect its citizens. These endless arguments are often well-reasoned, making it difficult to discern the true meaning of the religious right's intervention in American political life. The rationale appears to be a natural extension of a uniquely American discourse about freedom. This deceptive use of language can even be found in George W. Bush's description of himself as a "compassionate conservative." As Judith Stacey commented in a July 2001 issue of *The Nation,* "The bland rhetoric of inclusiveness and compassion makes it more difficult to mobilize against regressive policies." This dilemma, which I will return to later, has been abetted by our own naïveté as we struggle to understand changes in public perceptions about the role of religion in American society. In order to demystify the religious right, liberals have to break from the way they have been taught to think about religion and focus on the disparities between the democratic rhetoric of evangelical politics and the actual vision being proffered of a future theocratic society.

To tear off the shroud with which the new religious conservatism has disguised itself, let's begin with some very basic questions. First, how does one make sense of an escalating series of violent political events in which religious belief plays an important part? How do we evaluate the role of faith in accounting for an attack on an abortion clinic or Timothy McVeigh's lethal destruction of the federal building in Oklahoma City? How did a specific interpretation of Christianity lead the Freemen in Montana to declare their own national sovereignty? Is there a history of deliberation about the just use of violence in religious circles? Do Christian Patriot militias like the Freemen and individuals such as the now-deceased John Salvi emerge out of a vacuum? Or are their actions merely aberrations that express socially induced pathologies created by poverty, agitation, and media manipulation in an otherwise stable world?

During his trial for the murder of two abortion-clinic workers in Brookline, Massachusetts, John Salvi explained to the jury that he had acted out of fear of a conspiracy against the Catholic working class by Freemasons and the Illuminati. Salvi's lawyers argued that such statements were the products of a homicidal, paranoid disorder that they attributed to schizophrenia. When right-wing social-movement researcher Chip Berlet submitted evidence that Salvi's paranoid delusions were actually beliefs widely held by members of conservative Catholic organizations, the religious right, and the Christian Patriot movement, he was required to withhold the information from the trial.

The intentions of the Massachusetts Supreme Court in suppressing this information are open to question. One hypothesis is that it was a pragmatic decision: It would have been counter-productive to admit information as evidence that could have turned Salvi's prosecution into a high-profile political event. On the other hand, the judge may have indeed concluded that there was sufficient evidence to convict Salvi of murder, and that any additional evidence would simply have prolonged an inevitable conviction. But the issue is far more complex. Convicting an individual of a crime is not the same thing as alleging a greater conspiracy or convicting a worldview. Or is it?

A comprehensive analysis of the threat posed by the religious right must move beyond the liberal worldview that looks to the individual for the explanations of her or his actions. Social movements—religious or otherwise—provide narrative frameworks that encourage individuals to act in a particular manner, even when those individuals are clinically insane. The tragedy of the Salvi verdict is that it further neutralized the meaning of an act that was deliberately and inherently political. The reason we have difficulty understanding the politics of such desperate acts of violence is that we see them as being isolated from other seemingly disconnected events—such as the burning of the Waco compound or the standoffs with Identity Christians at Ruby Ridge and Jordan, Montana.

The extremism of the Branch Davidians, the Montana

Freemen, and fans of *The Turner Diaries* like Timothy McVeigh has been driven by a collectively nurtured fear of an impending social order. This fear has its roots in biblical apocalyptic literature in which prophets and apostles foretold the coming end of the world. These prophecies can be interpreted as desperate solutions to the political events of their respective historical conditions. Unable to influence political changes in Roman-occupied Palestine, for example, the author of Revelations expressed his desire to see the Roman regime eviscerated by the greater hand of God; no effective opposition existed to expel the Romans from the territory they occupied. Thus, the overthrow of Roman authority was conveyed as the end of the world in its entirety, an expression of the author's own frustrated desire for a change he and his people were powerless to bring about. In this manner, cultural narratives concretize our repressed desires and yearnings for a better world.

One problem with projecting frustrated utopian yearnings in this way is that it can inspire the creation of homicidal, paranoid political dispositions as a means of redressing collective disenfranchisement from the political process. For this reason, abortion-clinic workers can be murdered without the general public grasping how such acts are deeply political—regardless of their perpetrators' sanity or self-understanding. A lesson from the Salvi trial is that Christian conservatives are able to act politically but the public is not allowed to appreciate how their actions relate to their belief system. Why? Because liberal ideology denies the public the opportunity to place actions like those of Salvi within a greater social and historical context. Such obstructions of meaning serve to increase the accumulative power of those social movements which are responsible for inspiring crimes within a greater cultural narrative. Thus, it becomes very difficult to educate the public about why people engage in political activities above and beyond their subjective dispositions.

For those outside the religious sphere, the result is always the same: Individuals who deviate from social norms are understood to be acting outside of a standard of behavior in line with establishment definitions of good citizenship. Even though this interpretation is promoted by ostensibly liberal societies such as our own in order to dissuade people from antisocial activity, individuals and communities continue to engage in forms of social action arising from subversive cultural and political narratives which threaten the reigning ideology. The religious right's appeal to apocalyptic historical narratives is the ideological reservoir that nourishes its anti-establishment politics; apocalypticism always presupposes the fallen social order prior to the Rapture.

In liberal circles, however, it simply is not supposed to work that way: Religious politics violate the notion of spirituality as a private affair, and it shouldn't get any deeper than that. After all, the state—not the Bible—defines the political *reach* of religion. As necessary a check on the potential power of organized religion as this might be, it also prevents the secular from truly understanding the political dimensions of spirituality, irrespective of denominational affiliation. Consequently, liberals derive their concept of a de-politicized, private spirituality from the constitutional separation of church and state, not from scripture. In contrast with the authority and influence of a book more widely read than the American Constitution—the Bible—this liberal attitude provides a weak basis for the defense of the secular welfare state.

Progressives have traditionally thought of Christianity as a belief system that unreflectively legitimates the status quo. But this is not what has been happening over the past twenty-five years. Far from promoting the stability of the present social order, religious conservatives have been challenging it because they don't believe it is in their interest to continue supporting it. This scenario is further distorted when the religious right and its various permutations avoid representing themselves as anti-establishment. The Christian Coalition's alliance with the Republican Party and big business is a prime example. So is its narrative self-representation as a middle-class social movement committed to democratic, legislative politics.

When Operation Rescue disintegrated, the religious right began to make the transformation from a moral reform movement into a loosely defined network of quasi-revolutionary organizations united by their animosity toward the secular state. After Presidents Reagan and Bush (senior) proved unable to enact the legislative and constitutional changes which first the Moral Majority and then the Christian Coalition demanded in exchange for its support—e.g., overturning *Roe vs. Wade,* reintroducing prayer in public schools—members of the religious right began forming organizations dedicated to forcing abortion clinics out of business through civil disobedience campaigns. Lawsuits to protect access to clinics by Planned Parenthood, the American Civil Liberties Union, and the National Organization of Women, along with rulings by the US Supreme Court, effectively neutralized mainstream Christian activist groups.

Then something popped. Despite the fact that the religious right had put enough pressure on the state and civil society to sound its message, religious conservatives now perceived themselves as having advanced their agenda as far as possible within the confines of a bourgeois, constitutional democracy. Even though the Christian point of view was better represented than ever before, it could not fulfill its entire program by working *within* the system. As a consequence, religious conservatives followed the lead of many radical social movements of the 1960s and 1970s and started working outside of the state's legal and cultural protections.

The religious right began to reconfigure itself, not just strategically but institutionally and ideologically as well. It became increasingly radical as the rank-and-file realized the futility in their efforts to turn state institutions and popular culture around to reflect a Christian worldview. They began to blame the very nature of the secular state and its liberal, pluralistic ideologies for the dissolution of our communities, our national character, and our Judeo-Christian values.

It wasn't as though Christians had shied away from confronting the establishment in the past. Conservative religious intellectuals such as Francis Schaeffer, Gary North, and Rousas John Rushdoony had been identifying the institutional and ideological bankruptcy of liberal democracy since the heyday of the student movement in the mid-1960s. The difference was that counter-hegemonic strategies were now deemed inadequate unless they were backed up by the threat of force. Ever since federal injunctions placed limits upon the extent to which anti-abortion activists can demonstrate in front of clinics, former members of Operation Rescue have shown increasing tenacity in pursuing their agenda, beginning with the assassination of Dr. David Gunn by a Presbyterian minister in the early 1990s. As the Clinton administration and the judiciary continued to prosecute anti-abortion activists, increasing signs of paramilitary organizing emerged. These included the unearthing of terrorist manuals—from groups like The Free Militia and Army of God—providing scriptural legitimization for the use of violence, and instructions on how to manufacture and detonate crude homemade explosives.

The rise of religious paramilitancy was profoundly catalyzed by the government's siege of the Branch Davidian compound in Waco in 1993. Many evangelicals found the government's attack on the Mount Carmel compound to be proof of the irreconcilability of religious politics with secular democracy. The burning of Koresh's commmunity further proved to members of Christian Patriot militias that liberalism was *violently* opposed to religious forms of social organization. Biblical scholars and sociologists of religion such as James Tabor and Nancy Ammerman have focused their critiques of the government's handling of the affair on how ignorantly it disregarded the religious beliefs of the Branch Davidians. Few, however, have considered the degree to which the government's assault was symbolic of the secular state's misunderstanding of American religious politics in general. This is particularly apparent in the context of a growing social movement whose leadership has for years argued that the federal government's disestablishment clause actively discriminates against the civil rights of God-fearing, tax-paying Christians.

Judging from all the cries of "No More Wacos" by evangelical paramilitary organizations and militia leaders throughout the nineties, it seems evident that the violent suppression of a religious minority confirmed for many what their preachers and political leaders had been telling them all along. This illuminates the strong cross-pollination of Protestant evangelism with anti-government sentiment. The development of paramilitary forms of social organization to defend this hybrid speaks to a perfectly understandable fear that the events at Waco might be repeated. The renewal of hostilities between the state and deeply religious, end-time communities, including the standoff involving the Montana Freemen in 1996, indicated that the specter of another Waco loomed large throughout the decade.

This must be carefully considered, especially in light of the fact that one of the two greatest acts of terrorism in American history, the 1995 bombing of the Arthur R. Murrah Federal Building in Oklahoma City, was apparently carried out by two individuals associated with the Christian Patriot movement. Over a hundred and fifty state and federal employees were killed, ostensibly in retaliation for the burning of the Mount Carmel compound two years earlier. Other incidents such as the derailment of an Amtrak train in Arizona later that year by a group calling itself "The Sons of the Gestapo" were also said to be revenge attacks for the government's assault on the Branch Davidians. The letter left behind by the saboteurs in Waco, describing women in the compound performing the customary lighting of Sabbath candles just before the government's attack, enhanced the psychological impact that the assault had on collective evangelical insecurities. It is an image of religious ritual desecrated by the state.

Though the media cast David Koresh and his seventy-five immolated followers as cultists who, like John Salvi, white supremacist Randy Weaver, and the Montana Freeman's Leroy Schweitzer, were on the lunatic fringe of American religious life, such portrayals only obfuscate what marginal communities have in common with the evangelical mainstream: a radical apocalyptic worldview and a commitment to building a covenant community. The difference between mainstream political evangelicals and those evangelicals who live in intentional communities (often structured around the magnetism of preachers like Koresh) is only the manner in which charismatic authority and the maintenance of end-time worldviews are administratively organized. One of the means by which the religious right has built an ideologically coherent and identifiable political community is by continuously reminding the faithful that the metaphysical powers of the modern American nation-state are arrayed against Christians as part of the greater cosmic struggle between Satan and God. Just turn on your car radio and tune in to a local evangelical station to hear how those dastardly Feds are out to get the truly righteous.

Or, simply consider this conversation between Jerry Falwell and Pat Robertson following the destruction of New York's World Trade Center on September 11, 2001:

Jerry Falwell: The ACLU's got to take a lot of blame for this.
Pat Robertson: Well, yes.

> Jerry Falwell: And I know that I'll hear from them for this. But throwing God out successfully with the help of the federal court system, throwing God out of the public square, out of the schools . . . The abortionists have got to bear some burden for this because God will not be mocked. And when we destroy forty million little innocent babies, we make God mad. I really believe that the pagans, and the abortionists, and the feminists, and the gays and lesbians who are actively trying to make that an alternative lifestyle, the ACLU, People for the American Way, all of them who have tried to secularize America, I point the finger in their face and say, "You helped this happen."
> Pat Robertson: Well, I totally concur, *and the problem is we have adopted that agenda at the highest levels of our government.* [emphasis added]

Ensuing apologies and retractions notwithstanding, these hateful words on Robertson's television program, *The 700 Club,* two days after the attack, belie the sincerity of the religious right's description of their movement as an inclusive one founded on democratic principles.

Separatist communities like the Branch Davidians and the Montana Freemen are as much the products of the religious right as is the media empire of a Pat Robertson. No matter how transparent the message of Christian talk radio and the Christian alternative press may appear, it has been instrumental in allowing organizations like the Christian Coalition to form a political constituency within a highly differentiated, modern social context. The key is this message's ability to draw out Americans' deeply rooted fears of political disenfranchisement. Like many Americans, especially those in the downwardly mobile lower-middle class, right-wing Christians tend to be extremely worried about their future in a time of unprecedented socio-economic reorganization and de-industrialization. Now that the strategic foil of the communist menace is missing and conservatives are looking for new and convenient targets to revive the negative principle around which they have always organized, recasting economic insecurities in spiritual terms is a strikingly effective strategy. Given this context, it is not particularly surprising that the assault on the Waco compound became a confirmation of the evangelical movement's greatest apocalyptic fears. If we miss this meaning, we disregard the depth of evangelical piety and the extent to which people remain deeply socialized by traditional worldviews in the face of rapid change.

Over the past few decades, the computer has been a prime mover in this profound transformation. The computerization of society has had an unsettling effect on many American lives, making whole sectors of the workforce expendable, giving government and corporations unprecedented amounts of information about people, and opening the public's eyes to the diversity of lifestyles across the country and the world. Predictably, a large percentage of the population has experienced further alienation as a result. But there is another side to this transformation of everyday life that must be explored. As home computers became common in the 1980s, many Americans sought to overcome their fear of a programmed future by using their computers as a means of community-building on primitive, yet alluring "bulletin board systems." With the explosion of Internet culture in the 1990s, networks of like-minded individuals began to expand exponentially. These efforts at electronic community-building may appear to represent progress, but they are only "progressive" in a technological sense. Like any tool, the Internet is only as politically progressive as the people who use it. And quite a lot of the people who do use it are enemies of progressive politics. For example, a few years back I received a message from an online services provider that specialized in forwarding prayer requests to God through the Internet. According to the letter, for the mere price of ten dollars I could send an e-mail to the Almighty through my modem. This service would convert my prayer into speech, then project it up into the heavens, directly into God's own ear.

Why I was chosen to receive such a divine privilege is still unclear. Maybe I'd been visiting too many evangelical websites. In any event, as a result of being invited to participate in religious life on the Internet, I was able to familiarize myself with the intellectual workings of a very real community that, however archaic its beliefs, still has a lot to teach progressives about the political malleability of new technologies (i.e., how they can be used to enforce worldviews that seem antithetical to the political freedoms forever promised by high technology). Indeed, it would not be until the rise of Indymedia.org sites during the 1999 protests against the World Trade Organization in Seattle that the left would come close to approximating (but in far smaller numbers) the partisan Internet presence pioneered by right-wing religious and militia organizations during the mid-1990s.

The religious presence in cyberspace represents a deliberate effort on the part of evangelical and extremist Protestant political organizations to take advantage of the Web's potential for missionary activity, consensus building, and political education. The religious right's portion of virtual reality is divided into two principle areas: mainstream outlets, including a wide range of magazines like *Christianity Today*, news services, and discussion groups that are carried by major Internet providers such as America Online; and World Wide Web pages, which tend to be more explicitly partisan and activism-oriented, such as the Christian Coalition's site (www.cc.org), the early Christian Identity site (taken down recently, but partially archived at www.nizkor.org), and Pastor Pete Peters's long-running Scriptures for America (www.scripturesforamerica.org).

Unlike offline evangelical broadcasting, where one encounters more traditionally mainstream conservative opinions, religious online services and web pages provide us with a sampling of the entire spectrum of evangelical politics. In the Religion and Ethics forum on AOL during the mid-1990s, for instance, Elder Ronald C. Schoedel III of Christian Identity frequently contributed pro-Nazi tracts dismissing the Holocaust in tandem with "Jew World Order" conspiracy theories—adding to the traditional stew of homophobic, pro-life, and family-values literature we tend to associate with organizations like the Christian Coalition. If you've ever wondered how far a leap it would be for an evangelical radio talk-show host to move from gay-bashing to anti-Semitic tirades, here's your opportunity to witness the logical continuum of conservative Christian politics. Schoedel's contributions were just the beginning. It wasn't always so transparent.

The Internet has allowed traditional religious broadcasters to work around the prohibitions that liberalism has historically imposed on right-wing programming. As early as the 1940s, Theodor Adorno wrote that it was difficult to discern the fascist politics of radio ministers because American democratic ideology had evolved certain restraints. He theorized that breaking these taboos threatened to jeopardize the subversive activities of pro-fascist preachers of that era, such as the pioneering radio minister Father Charles Coughlin. But the twenty-six years since the end of the Vietnam War have witnessed a discrediting of liberalism that has weakened these prohibitions. The collapse of the welfare state, the endless promulgation of rhetoric about the inherent value of the free market, and the rise of violent anti-statist protest movements have played major roles in eroding the institutional basis of liberal proscriptions. The taboos that Adorno wrote about have been supplanted by a discursive ideology of free expression perfectly in step with the new base of economic production, information technology.

The openness that we associate with Internet communications has nothing to do with the physical medium of cyberspace itself. This frankness of interaction already exists in other broadcast mediums including talk radio, television, and rock and roll—even with the liberal language constrictions in place. The reactionary, common-sense populism of talk radio hosts preceded the "ideal speech situation" we call the Internet by a long shot. Rush Limbaugh, Bob Larson, and like-minded conservative radio personalities were hosting inflammatory talk shows for years. Although the Clinton administration waged a smear campaign after the Oklahoma bombing against right-wing organizations that publish their opinions on the Internet, the political potential of cyberspace wasn't really breaking new ground. The Internet merely added new layers of right-wing propaganda to a media landscape already saturated with it.

Before we attribute utopian possibilities for communication to the Internet, we ought to consider why people seem to be expressing themselves more openly these days. The creeping illness we call the religious media, along with its increasing visibility and influence, is inseparable from the new openness we attribute to American media culture in general. Like all other aspects of popular culture, contemporary religious broadcasting is symptomatic of a collective nervous breakdown; the emergence of formerly suppressed discourses like those of the religious right must be read as one aspect of a widespread call for help accompanying the demise of liberalism. The religious right stands out only because it has been particularly successful at filling the void left in liberalism's wake. Its ability to take advantage of all the propagandistic opportunities offered by the new communications technologies is an indication of this success.

This use of the latest technology for reactionary purposes has a strong precedent in the history of Western civilization. As Walter

Benjamin once stated, religion persists despite the advent of mass production because the fragmentation that late capitalism creates in our lives forces us to find ways of preserving some sense of transcendence in the face of modern industry's secularizing impulses. When Father Tom tried to turn me on to the presence of God in the formulas of high-school math, he was demonstrating his own quest for transcendence in the building blocks of modern thought. The rituals of the Branch Davidians and other so-called cults are more fully elaborated examples of this phenomenon.

In the religious colonization of the Internet, we see the very same process at work, as the democratic promise of the new communications infrastructure is overwhelmed by religion's ability to reproduce ritual values in cyberspace. But the evangelical baptism of the Internet goes even deeper. According to scripture, God created the world out of speech. Cyberspace thereby allows the religious right to use language to achieve cultural dominance in an information-based economy. When contemplating what kind of future the Christian Coalition has in store for us, we would do well to reflect on the virtual model that the evangelical community has already built alongside the information superhighway.

The celebration of the Internet's potential to permit transparent communication between alienated subjects perfectly illustrates how poorly the burnt-out shell of liberal ideology has dealt with technological innovation. This ideology presupposes that technology will liberate us from an undemocratic reality where it is impossible to speak freely to one another. From this laissez-faire perspective, the Internet opens up vast possibilities for overcoming the social differences and class conflicts that we experience in everyday life because it disguises us from one another in the act of communication. A perfect example of this optimism is the claim Apple Computer founder and CEO Steve Jobs made a few years back that web pages demonstrate cyberspace's democratic nature by giving individuals the ability to create personalized home pages as large and elegant as that of any multinational corporation. These days, of course, the gulf between corporate and personal websites is widening, as the increasing use of high-bandwidth visuals makes it hard for individuals to compete with the corporate dollar. But Jobs's utopian reading of the Internet is still mirrored in countless arguments and, predictably, advertisements, even as the NASDAQ tries to recover the luster it had in the late 1990s. And although the Internet bubble began to burst in mid-2000 and hasn't shown any signs of recovery, we still subscribe to the naïve dreams that kept it aloft through most of the Clinton era.

The liberal doctrine of social equality has never been so aesthetic: Because we are able to represent ourselves as equals in cyberspace we can now overcome class differences in our actual lives. In effect, Steve Jobs and his fellow high-tech boosters reduce the post-capitalist vision of utopia to the mechanical will of technology. Such visions of post-industrial society acknowledge our incapacity to will a better world into existence. In its search to find a new institutional infrastructure, liberalism takes root in the minds of technocrats like Jobs who turn the Internet into a museum as they seek to recreate the disintegrating social conditions that gave rise to the Enlightenment vision of social equality.

In an issue of *Wired* magazine published during the height of Internet mania, Maurice Berger argued that the Internet provides us with the possibility for opening up a real conversation about racial issues, forcing individuals to speak candidly. As a social space free from the constraints of society and tradition, he reasoned, online discourse offers the chance to resolve social conflicts by allowing us to observe how it is we really think and feel about one another. It helps us see racist language "for the bullshit it really is when spelled out onscreen."

In an ideal world, all forms of reactionary discourse would be emptied of their supposed truth content by the force of a better argument. The belief that racism can be overcome through speech is a sign of frustration over our inability to concretely resolve such problems. The social basis for such abstract resolutions of real political dilemmas is a primary feature of liberal cyber-ideology. In a *New York Times* article from the same period as Berger's piece in *Wired,* Edward Rothstein mistakenly described this Internet-inspired consciousness as one in which we are free to define ourselves *performatively* since the ahistorical content of cyberspace permits us to create a virtual society without precedent. It then becomes possible, he suggests, to overcome problems of race and class without recourse to the forms of identification conferred upon us by history. By redefining ourselves as a discursive citizenry, we empower ourselves with a kind of symbolic capital that we need to survive in an economy in which language has become the raw material of production.

What is lost in the continuous struggle to adapt to new modes of production is the memory of how we are fundamentally constituted by historical forces. In our celebration of the Internet, we have forgotten the dangers that technology has historically presented. Religious online services, bulletin boards, and web pages are cases in point. Faxing God the text of our spoken prayers in order to alleviate our real, this-worldly suffering is only the tip of the iceberg. No matter how diligently individuals who are convinced of the Internet's potential strive to escape history, they will always be confronted with forces like the religious right that are proactively intent on making new technology subservient to antiquity.

Ironically, the progressive view that communications technology is a vehicle for consciousness-raising is shared by the religious right. Whereas well-meaning liberals see cyberspace as an image of the ideal *polis*, the religious right has turned cyberspace into an effective means for advancing the construction of a technological theocracy. Perhaps it's because the weight of history is on their side. Unlike the secular left, the religious community has spent over half a century perfecting its use of electronic broadcasting. This should not be forgotten. When politics have been driven so far right that Republicans can convincingly claim that National Public Radio and the *New York Times* constitute the "leftist" counterpart to the right's media apparatus, we may be tempted to declare defeat before even beginning to battle.

Liberals have transposed their innocent commitment to ethical neutrality to the brave new world of the Internet without recognizing that while information is the new Platonic capital, there is nothing neutral about its content: Truth is always partisan. What is so disturbing about Steve Jobs's notion of virtual equality is that it confines human agency to the level of *representation*. This leaves liberals subject to the tyranny of information. The religious right is able to avoid this problem because it contextualizes technological change within an all-encompassing cultural narrative derived from scripture. If the left simply learned to contextualize its fetishization of technology within a historical context, it would cease to project its own repressed desire for social equality onto the very technologies the religious right is using to defeat it.

Evangelical propaganda in cyberspace is designed to spur the believer into action. Evangelical web pages reveal the true meaning of radio and television ministers' coded phrases, such as "forces of darkness" or "the war going on between the children of light and the armies of evil." When the Christian Coalition first got its website up and running in the mid-nineties, for example, it posted excerpts from texts such as liberal scholar Robert McAfee Brown's *Religion and Violence*. According to the Coalition's editors at that time, Brown's work delineates the components of Catholic "just war" doctrine:

1. The war must be declared by a legitimate authority.
2. A war cannot be just if it is waged with the wrong intention, such as the desire to secure vengeance or to satisfy lust for domination.
3. The war must be undertaken only as a last resort.
4. The war must be waged on the basis of proportionality.
5. The war must have a reasonable chance of success.
6. The war must be waged with all moderation possible.

The Coalition web page then summarized Brown's account of the history of Christian violence—beginning with the recruitment of Christians into the Legion Fulminata in the second century, proceeding to the Crusades, and wrapping up with a summary of Jenny Teichman's *Pacifism and Just War.* The posted history addresses the doctrinal rationale for killing unbelievers—despite the prohibitions placed on priests and monks who engage in acts of violence. The purpose of this posting was clear. Within the context of the Christian Coalition's activities, it responded to the theological soul-searching going on in evangelical America's conscience as right-wing Christians sought to justify the use of violence against abortion clinics and, more broadly, the secular state.

While stopping short of explicitly endorsing the use of violence in constructing a theocratic society, such postings school fundamentalist net-surfers in the "legitimate" historical precedents for Christians taking up arms against the government. Such extreme acts, after all, must always have adequate theological justification. There are no ambiguous references to abstract demonic forces or racist innuendoes designed to facilitate a feeling of in-group solidarity. What we get instead is an implicit acknowledgment by the Christian Coalition, as in the example above, that it does not condemn violent means of seeking power, regardless of its commitment to participating in democratic electoral politics. The fact that the Christian Coalition once positioned itself in a leadership role for such purposes is very revealing, particularly in light of Brown's statement that "the war must be declared by a legitimate authority." The Christian Coalition wanted its web page readers to know that it would, if necessary, serve as the vanguard of a new evangelical insurrection.

Given the proliferation of Christian-identified militia organizations throughout the country during the mid-nineties, the Christian Coalition's forays into the justification of violence suggest that there might have been more affinities between these nationalist groups than was ever publicly recognized. Conversely, the implication that the Christian Coalition had the theological right to leadership of such a struggle can also be read as an attempt to draw in those disenfranchised Christians who belonged to para-religious revolutionary organizations like the White Aryan Resistance and the National Alliance. Even though many of these non-evangelical groups regarded organizations like the Christian Coalition with suspicion for being far too friendly to Jews and big business, it would have been difficult for the Coalition to miss the similar revolutionary spirit in their Odin-worshipping comrades, not to mention a shared commitment to creating an ethnically pure moral community.

For those inclined to dismiss such right-wing literature as a corrupt politicization of a Judeo-Christian tradition that preaches an ideology of love, Internet ministers such as Pastor Pete Peters of *Scriptures for America* have a disturbing reply. During the mid 1990s, Peters's website proudly declared that such politics articulate the heart of the Gospel message. In "The Bible: Handbook for Survivalists, Racists, Tax Protesters, and Right-Wing Extremists," Peters argued that the Christian rhetoric of charity and forgiveness is actually a distortion of the true Gospel message, because in reality, "God is no respecter of persons." Peters explained that the archetype for the right-wing Christian is found in such characters as Noah, the proto-survivalist whom God instructed to build an ark in order to survive; and Phineas, who heeded God's prohibition on race-mixing and interreligious marriages. Peters cites other Bible passages to support his contention that the political theory of Christianity is inherently conservative, particularly when it comes to legitimizing racism.

While many Christians would go to great pains to distinguish themselves from these populist theologians, the homepages of both *Scriptures for America* and the Christian Coalition illustrate, in their own distinct ways, how the new religious conservatism is drawing upon a fairly literal reading of scripture to justify its reactionary politics. We must remember that history is filled with examples of people mining complex and ambiguous traditions for their worst qualities. And while those same traditions have also motivated outstanding humanitarians and progressive activists, they are by no means immune to reactionary appropriation. In this respect, religious tradition is an awful lot like technology.

The religious right's presence on the Internet is a wake-up call to those of us who continue to believe that cyberspace represents a post-historical world where we can recreate ourselves on our own terms. The evangelical colonization of the Internet disproves such blissful illusions. Hopefully, once the transition period to the new mode of production is over and the Internet becomes more commonplace, we'll stop imbuing it with utopian dreams of self-realization and social justice.

Beyond the realm of the Internet, the religious right has often demonstrated itself to be more media-savvy than its liberal opponents. Whereas representatives of mainstream media conglomerates have consistently downplayed the role that culture plays in a nation's political landscape, the ideologues of the Christian insurgency see culture to be of paramount importance, recognizing its transformative power. They are fully aware that the means of communication can be employed for any number of purposes, and are not lulled into passivity by any conviction that media is inherently liberal. For the religious right, radio, television, and the Internet are battlegrounds, what progressives are fond of calling "spaces of contestation."

One of the most interesting examples of the religious right's media-savvy was its struggle against the imposing monolith of the Disney Corporation, which came to a head in 1996 and 1997. During that period, a consummate icon of "family values" became the epitome of evil for the religious right. The once-unimpeachable producer of children's entertainment, which has functioned historically as the equivalent of an advertising firm for everything from American imperialism to German automobile manufacturers, was charged with the crime of promoting homosexuality as a result of its support of same-sex partner benefits, Gay and Lesbian Days at Disneyland, and, most shocking of all, its endorsement of comedian Ellen DeGeneres's coming out publicly on her otherwise highly unremarkable sitcom, *Ellen*.

The Southern Baptist Convention had been warning Disney for over a year that its sixteen-million-strong denomination would boycott the company if it did not change its attitude toward homosexuality, both in its film and television productions and in its hiring practices. Finally, tensions between Disney and the SBC reached a fever pitch when church leaders introduced a motion calling for the ban. On June 18, 1997, the boycott was adopted, and many other Christian denominations in the US sounded their voices in support.

Although the Southern Baptist Convention took the initiative in its attack on Disney, several denominations—led by the agitation of the infamous American Family Association and other powerful groups that inhabit the greater religious right—were also active in forging the boycott. After the Republicans lost the 1996 presidential election, the Christian Coalition, under attack by the Federal Election Commission for purported voter fraud, had to find a new cause to reconstitute the voting constituency that it had built up over the past five years. What better a method for keeping members focused on transforming society after an electoral defeat than by launching a moral crusade? Charging that America's number-one producer of family entertainment was, in fact, a purveyor of "anti-family" ideologies was a crafty way of refocusing the revolutionary motivation in the movement's depressed ranks.

Nothing could have provided a better target than an instantly recognizable icon like the Disney Corporation, which was deviating from mainstream definitions of gender orientation by presenting marginal ones as equal. If played right, such a crisis could even be profitable! Somehow, if it could be proven to God-fearing, *Fantasia*-watching, downwardly mobile suburban consumers that Disney was in collusion with Satan to make homosexuality a legitimate lifestyle option, then alternative religious entertainment conglomerates like Pat Robertson's own Christian Broadcasting Network might become the rightful inheritors of Disney's market share. No matter what the political outcome of the boycott, it could still be a boon for the Christian entertainment industry. In an era in which the Promise Keepers—a father-son Christian organization—can pack stadiums with its rallies, it may be facile to ignore the economic side of the equation.

Fundamentalist marketing strategies aside, the real problem for the religious right was Disney's use of its media dominance to reconcile homosexuality with an established cultural order that also includes Christianity. As obvious as this may seem, it's this subtext of Disney's endorsement of homosexuality that made evangelical ideologues truly nervous. They feared the establishment of ideological equivalence, an insidious prospect for any group accustomed to having a symbolic monopoly on establishment lifestyle orientations. If there are narrative possibilities for legitimating the status quo beyond a tradition rooted in American Protestantism, the religious right's control of the morality question therefore threatens to slip away.

To fully appreciate the significance of evangelical anger at Disney, one has to take into account the degree to which some religious faiths are organized around repressing sexual desire in order to channel it into appropriate economic behavior. Telling Christians that such forms of repression are no longer necessary is like saying that their labor is no longer valued—that they are, figuratively speaking, *unemployed*. If the labor of a person who has broken free of this repression—or never experienced it in the first place—can prove more valuable than the labor of a God-fearing Christian who forswears earthly pleasures, the Protestant ethic must no longer apply. Homosexuals, sex radicals, and other so-called deviants who participate as equals in the labor force contradict the belief that it is necessary to hold your desire in check to succeed in the world. Frequently, these "outsiders" hold professional positions that pay three or four times more than a working-class job in the heartland. At least, that's how conservative Christians tend to see matters. Their intolerance is rooted in more than religious belief; it also expresses deep-seated economic anxieties. And despite what free-market economists will tell you, these anxieties promote not rational decision-making, but a desire to punish those who are deemed responsible for destabilizing the social order.

It is this economic dimension to homophobia that progressives need to comprehend. Every time political and cultural institutions find themselves in the position of appearing more inclusive—ethnically, spiritually, or sexually—progressives are caught in a double bind. They want the system to acknowledge the legitimacy of all citizens, not only as consumers in need of market variety, but as people who vote, pay taxes, and inhabit the middle class.

The desire to escape discrimination, however, to somehow see one's uniqueness represented as normal in the greater cultural order, should not come at the expense of ignoring the political and social history of an institution like Disney. When corporations show increased signs of tolerance—sponsoring Gay Days, giving artists the freedom in certain, albeit highly controlled instances to come out on national television—it doesn't mean that such institutions have suddenly become egalitarian. They haven't. Corporations like Disney continue to perform the same ideological functions as before. The difference is that they do so within the context of a market economy that tries to maintain a liberal façade. The acceleration of economic inequality and social injustice can be concealed behind images of inclusiveness. Disney's feel-good contributions to our cultural firmament provide a cover for both the labor practices of the conglomerate and the fundamental heartlessness of today's free market.

Like most progressives, I have struggled to strike a balance between my condemnation of the profit motive and my realization that tolerance can be profitable. When the monolith seems inflexible, you take what you can get; for that brief moment, you breathe a little more freely. It's easy to see why some continue to mistake the part for the whole: People become so starved for equality that after receiving a few measly moments of recognition, they either find ways of living with the remaining inequities or they become realists, renouncing their former dream of total liberation as an unrealistic fantasy.

Such admonitions are not meant to diminish the legitimate experience of exhilaration that accompanies every victory in the struggle for equality—even if that victory is confined to the realm of representation. Rather, the point is to recognize that the liberalization of mass culture is not synonymous with *political* equality, even if a parallel liberalization on the labor side of the equation puts additional corporate pressure on the state to legislatively guarantee equity in the work place. It becomes incumbent on the virtually integrated to develop a double consciousness—one that sees the strategic advantages of moving up the media ladder without forgetting that this progress is still restricted to the world of entertainment.

Religious conservatives are very sensitive to these struggles because their faith forces them to negotiate a similar balancing act between lived and desired realities. What they don't want is for the culture industry to disclose possibilities for sexual fulfillment incompatible with their own worldview; they fear it might lead to a spillover into real life. If homosexuality becomes an accepted media lifestyle orientation, it might then become a legislatively acceptable one—secured through the same kinds of struggles for recognition in which Christians engage. What motivates denominations like the Southern Baptist Convention to protest so loudly about Disney's policies is a desire to retain a *perceived* historical monopoly over such processes. They are unable—or unwilling—to recognize that mass producers of culture like Disney erode the hegemony of traditional worldviews all the time.

The culture industry's *raison d'être* is pushing new product, without any deference to tradition beyond the marketing department's desire to revive commodity lines that have been performing poorly. From this perspective, reaching out to gays and lesbians is in keeping with the industry's own "tradition" of putting profits first. Because the openly gay and lesbian demographic is a lot bigger than it used to be, media conglomerates cannot ignore it as they once did.

Disney's refusal to prioritize family values over the profit motive epitomizes the moral decline that the religious right fears. Significantly, callers to evangelical talk radio during the controversy stirred their intolerance of the "homosexual lifestyle" into a cocktail of beliefs old and new. "Disney has been taken over by homosexual *Jewish* activists," one caller complained. If gays and lesbians form a community that requires equal employment opportunities, living middle-class lifestyles that can be built into situation comedies, something must obviously have been *forgotten*. Not just Christ, but his nemeses: Jews, Satan, what have you. To be sure, this is mind-numbingly circular reasoning, but it is also incredibly commonplace, typifying the manner in which people with conservative religious worldviews react to historical change.

Social transformations are time and again interpreted as mythic recyclings of the past, whether it is history simply repeating itself or the reincarnation of despots from antiquity. Regardless, there's always a new King Herod to contend with. This means that there never really is a new "present," at least insofar as rank-and-file evangelicals are concerned. They are at the mercy of their ministers and political leadership, who, while fully able to discriminate between King Herod as a historical figure and King Herod as a character in a political allegory, do not explain this distinction to their followers. As a result, the devout are condemned to living in an intractable present that they are not encouraged to distinguish from an eternally recurring past. This makes it that much more difficult to teach people of traditional religious backgrounds to be more accepting of difference.

I think this is what has made the moral crusade against Disney so compelling to me. In essence, the Southern Baptist Convention and other religious groups were asking their membership to confront the distinctive features of present-day corporate multiculturalism without having prepared them to independently assess those distinctive features. They were practically forcing the rank-and-file to contemplate gender orientation, media representation, and labor. Can you think of a better education in contemporary politics? Most liberal arts institutions would be hard-pressed to offer undergraduate courses that teach that kind of neo-Marxist savvy. In this sense, the church is occasionally its own worst enemy: During cultural transitions, the church encourages the faithful to violate the terms of their own intellectual bondage. The lesson here is fascinating: Education is inevitably corrosive, particularly when it instructs people to interpret history on their own terms. It's called *involuntary secularization,* and it's the best friend that the left has in these trying times.

This doesn't necessarily mean that progressives ought to give up engaging critically with fundamentalists, because the logical course of capitalist development should eventually turn them into reasonable, possibly even sexually liberated people. But it is of utmost importance that those involved in struggles against religious conservatism grasp the whole picture and avoid indulging in the snotty hyperbole that many educated radicals tend to proffer, speaking about religious people as though they were backwards or stupid. Many of the people involved in the religious right are not ignorant so much as alienated. Like many minorities and people of color in the United States, they are disenfranchised. Their "backwards" worldview, for all of its inconsistency and prejudice, represents an attempt to compensate for their exclusion from decision-making.

It's clear from the Disney example that progressives have still not found an adequate means of confronting the new religious politics. When the Disney boycott was first announced, the most popular proposal from liberals was simply to buy Disney stock and support Disney products in order to compensate the company for the lost investments. Whether by going to see *George of the Jungle* or by picking up a pair of *Hercules* shoelaces, progressives were supposed to *buy buy buy.* If there's no threat to Disney's financial stability, according to this logic, the firm will continue to recognize same-sex relations. There are several problems with this strategy. To begin with, it repeats the same old liberal tactic of throwing money at social crises to try and cure problems that unfortunately have their roots in class conflict. If the strategy of liberal investment in a firm like Disney accomplishes anything, it is to verify that toleration of sexual difference in a corporate environment makes for good marketing.

The trade-off is simple: By investing in Disney to protect its recognition of same-sex partnerships, we destroy the universal implications of gay liberation by aligning it with big business and with the class conflicts perpetuated in the name of profit. This, in turn, transforms sexual politics into identity politics precisely by divorcing the sexual from the economic. After all, Disney is the fifth largest media monopoly in the world (in 1997, during the period of the SBC boycott, it was ranked second), one that is openly hostile to labor and routinely promotes reactionary family-values ideologies through its film and music subsidiaries.

This "alternative" act of consumption is quite literally—for lack of a better term—a sell-out. Still, many progressives believe that investing in culture is an important way to protect our universal freedoms. This is a defensive attitude that requires throwing money at problems that were largely caused by issues pertaining to money in the first place. Moreover, this approach obscures the larger struggle for a truly inclusive democratic society. Democracy must be continually fought for, especially in market-driven societies; the economy is never innately democratic. Each fight for tolerance and inclusion is an attempt to reform society against the market's anarchic tendencies. But without an accompanying political philosophy, without any sense of an alternative political order, all attempts to promote democracy will be futile.

In this regard, the recent merger of the most prominent gay media outlets, including *The Advocate, Out* magazine, Gay.com,

PlanetOut, and Alyson (a leading gay publisher) into a single huge conglomerate is a bit ominous. Doug Ireland opined in *The Nation* that "the aggressive search for advertising dollars from corporate America, which is increasingly targeting the gay market, has undoubtedly contributed to the homogenization and depoliticization of the gay press."

This is not meant to downplay the necessity of the local struggles surrounding corporations like Disney. There's nothing wrong with supporting the subversion of one of the most reactionary institutions in the culture industry so that it becomes a principal source for images of a sexually liberated society. This kind of activity can facilitate greater forms of cultural tolerance and political inclusiveness in the future. This is exactly what religious moralists are so fucking worried about. Who knows what kind of social upheaval will eventually stem from prime-time portraits of gays and lesbians leading normal, loving lives?

While it would be difficult to gauge the exact impact of the Southern Baptist Convention's failure to halt Disney's bold move into a sexually inclusive new millennium on rank-and-file church activists, it can be assumed that there was immense disappointment. At the very least, such frustration would be expected to serve as an incentive for the greater religious right to redouble its efforts to over-determine the nature of popular discourse about acceptable forms of sexual behavior in America. Indeed, the crisis that befell the White House later that year surrounding President Clinton's extramarital affair with a female intern of Jewish descent undoubtedly led to a certain sense of evangelical vindication. The religious right nearly brought down the government, and they were able to cast inter-religious sexual relations as perverted and threatening to the nuclear family. But given their failure to halt Disney, the Lewinsky affair actually highlighted the push and pull that evangelicals have to endure in their attempts to colonize American culture.

For every victory, there's often a pronounced letdown. Sometimes, the experience of failure can be so tremendous that one questions how the devout can persevere. The answer, of course, is that not everyone does.

It used to be that certain denominations and traditions of theological reflection could interpret failure as a reflection of the will of God. Nothing happens on earth without *His* consent, even the existence of evil. However, this doesn't always mean that the devoted can find a way of coping with all the despair. Accepting the existence of evil might also entail taking leave of it so that no more compromises have to be struck and no more battles have to be fought.

Following this reasoning, the mass suicide on Good Friday, 1998, in a mansion in an affluent suburb of San Diego, should not have caused such widespread astonishment. Like many recent events in American religious history, it represented a powerful indictment of the poverty of contemporary life. All of the epistemological ingredients for a dystopian verdict on technological and cultural progress were there. Heaven's Gate was an end-time community centered around the leadership of a couple claiming to be genderless aliens.

The group was fueled by a traditional millennial eschatology of Christian derivation, which emphasized rejecting the mind, body, and sensuality. And it was populated by ascetic web-page designers who all wore the same clothes and haircuts and frequently followed their male leader Do's example by castrating themselves. They referred to their bodies as "containers" and packed overnight bags with clothes and toilet accessories, waiting for a space ship to take them to a better world.

As usual, the whole affair was distorted by the media. Experts on cults were consulted by major news organizations. Pastors and theologians were asked for their opinions; like clockwork, they reduced the tragedy to a pathological outburst by a dynamic madman suffering from his own particular brand of fascist megalomania. It was the same old story with the same resolution. First there was Jonestown, then Waco. Now it was San Diego. In time-honored fashion, I turned on the radio as soon as I heard about what had happened and tuned into the local Christian talk show to hear their dissection of the mass suicide. "We've been warning the public about the dangers of cults for years," one noted evangelical talk-show host remarked, "and the authorities never listen to us. This should serve as a warning that the church has to start protecting Americans from themselves the way God commanded Christ to protect us."

The overwhelming public consensus about the Heaven's Gate community was that its members committed suicide because they were a cult, and cults always kill themselves. The implication, of course, was that *real* religious people don't behave irrationally. However, the Heaven's Gate theology, for all intents and purposes, is a Christian theology. In fact, it's so steeped in classic neo-Platonist religious motifs that it's almost Gnostic. Just because Heaven's Gate substituted a flying saucer for Jesus Christ doesn't mean its members' beliefs were significantly different from those found in certain strands of American Protestantism; they were actually quite similar. But the religious right—this time working, ironically, with "allies" in the mainstream media—did everything in its power to hide the family resemblance.

For years, mainstream American Christians and therapists alike have drawn a distinction between cultism and religion, deflecting attention from certain Protestant beliefs—particularly those which reject the world out of disgust with its corruption, its lack of meaning, and its emptiness. Like the members of the Heaven's Gate cult, many Christians see death and the second coming as a means to annihilate the fallen world which traps all of us. They truly possess a death wish. As with the extremism of individuals like Father Tom Goman, John Salvi, and Timothy McVeigh, the consequences of this line of thinking can be remarkably destructive. This is not some diffuse desire for personal and political transformation, but a will to bring death to the existing social order.

We have to learn to come to terms with the psychological undercurrents which inform all of our spiritual dispositions, especially in a country as nihilistic as America. We need to stop taking for granted that spiritual phenomena are separate from material ones, and recall that every aspect of culture—religious or otherwise—emerges largely out of a rich, historically self-conscious Protestant society. The charge of cultism is a reflection of the guilty conscience of certain forms of spirituality that worship death as though it were a cure for a world beyond changing. Once we've begun to make these basic connections, we'll be able to better understand developments such as the Heaven's Gate suicide. Only then can we start forming our own opinions about the events instead of believing what we're told by a society in denial of its own suicidal impulses.

❖

If there's one central message I want to get across, it's that religion and, more specifically, radical Protestant theology, play a far bigger role in the contemporary United States than most commentators are willing to admit. It's a role that needs to be acknowledged and closely examined if we are to make sense of the present social order and the forces working to undermine it.

Declaring January 20, 2001 to be a "National Day of Prayer," George "Dubya" Bush sanctified his presidential swearing in as though he were an emissary dispatched directly from the heavens above. Asking Americans to "gather together in our homes and places of worship to pray alone and together, and offer thanksgiving to God for all the blessings of this great and good land," Bush waxed holy. He continued, "I ask Americans to bow our heads in humility before our Heavenly Father, a God who calls us not to judge our neighbors but to love them, to ask His guidance upon our nation and its leaders in every level of government." Bush's gender-specific uses of "Heavenly Father" and "His" were a dead giveaway that his "inclusive" call for prayer was disingenuous.

Subsequently, our new president demonstrated what the political end-result of his demand for government-mandated piety would be. First, he called for a "declaration of independence for the unborn," stating that "declarations of independence [are] not for just the strong, the independent, or the healthy. They are for everyone, including unborn children." Then, during his first official day in office (which, not so coincidentally, was the twenty-eighth anniversary of the *Roe vs. Wade* decision legalizing abortion), Bush suspended $540 million of federal funding for overseas family planning and abortion counseling services.

Of course, it's nothing new to hear an American politician invoking a holy mandate, particularly if he or she is a Republican. Furthermore, funding for overseas family planning and abortion counseling services was also suspended during the 1980s by Presidents Reagan and Bush, only to be restored by the Democrats in 1993. What distinguishes Bush's actions from those of his immediate Republican predecessors is that they reveal an agenda he had kept hidden during the election campaign: his quest to circumvent the constitution's separation of church and state.

The second religious policy announcement Bush made during the first week of his presidency addressed his newly formed Office of Faith-Based and Community Initiatives. The purpose of the Office is to distribute federal tax dollars to religious groups to provide an array of social services now being administered by government agencies and secular nonprofit organizations. However, the authority of the office is designed to extend far beyond simply disbursing funds; it is also supposed to be a moral force within the government. The Office of Faith may be greatly assisted through the establishment of satellite oversight centers at the Departments of Justice, Education, Labor, Health and Human Services, and Urban Development. This is presumably intended to ensure that these agencies cooperate with Dubya's new activist religious branch of the White House.

According to the *Guardian's* Ed Vulliamy, $24 billion in taxpayer money could be transferred to religious organizations for social work over the next several years. Anticipating criticism of the partisan religious nature of such an officially sanctioned hand-out—the bigger the faith, the more money it would stand to get—Bush appointed John J. DiIulio, a Catholic, and Stephen Goldsmith, a Jew, as directors of the Office of Faith with the notion that the distinctions between their beliefs would promote equitable funding decisions. Unfortunately, when it comes to policy-making, religious diversity is no guarantee of social justice.

DiIulio, for example, is a political scientist who, despite identifying himself as a moderate Democrat, has been a leading advocate of increased prison construction. He is also co-author (with former education secretary William J. Bennett and current Bush administration drug czar John P. Walters) of *Body Count,* a now-out-of-print book about the war on crime and how religion can be an effective means to combat the acceleration of youth violence and drug abuse. Equally disturbing is co-director Goldsmith's track record as a former prosecutor and two-term mayor of Indianapolis, during which time he made a mark by privatizing sewage treatment. This diversity of faith amounts to very little, except for the insulting reassurance that the Jew will make sure the Gentile does not show too much deference to his brethren, and vice versa. What counts are the political prejudices that both men share—in this case, a profound commitment to privatizing federal welfare services. (In August 2001, DiIulio resigned from the post; some pundits speculate that working with hard-line evangelicals alligned with the Bush administration was more than he could stomach.)

Clearly, such policy initiatives this early in Bush's presidency are radical in their implications. Anticipating lawsuits attacking the government's partnering with religious organizations as unconstitutional, the Bush administration rammed through its appointment to the office of Attorney General of a legislator who could sustain such an assault: Christian Coalition poster child John Ashcroft, a former Senator and governor of Missouri. Ashcroft is a fairly devout Pentecostal, well-known for his support of a variety of religious causes—from the reintroduction of prayer in public schools and the elimination of the National Endowment for the Arts to a constitutional amendment outlawing abortion (even in cases of rape and incest). In 1996, Ashcroft authored the "Charitable Choice" provision tacked onto President Clinton's Welfare Reform Act, prohibiting states from discriminating against religious groups when funding social-service programs while allowing them to discriminate, on the basis of their religious beliefs, who would be eligible for such social assistance. In other words, basic human needs are no longer the sole criteria for government assistance, and welfare may be more readily withheld on the basis of race, gender, or religious orientation.

Although he denies any intention of imposing his beliefs on others, Ashcroft has also stated that it is the government's role to legislate morality. So where's the rub? It comes with the interchangeability of words like "religion" and "morality" in the vocabularies of politicians who are supposed to honor the secular code of our constitution. The fact is that Ashcroft has always promoted his religious beliefs in the form of legislative initiatives. Given how hard he fought to *not* enforce constitutionally mandated desegregation in St. Louis when he was governor (Ashcroft was criticized by Judge William Hungate as an obstructionist), it is difficult to imagine that he will heed the constitution's disestablishment clause when the Bush administration is sued—as it surely will be—for transgressing the boundaries that separate church and state. Laurie Goodstein of the *New York Times* quoted Ashcroft as saying that moral judgements rely on God, scriptures, and faith. If the nation's top lawyer believes that faith trumps legal codes, he will therefore be put in the position of trying to reform the law accordingly. This is exactly why Bush named him Attorney General.

Bush's appointment of Ashcroft epitomizes the legal savvy that his administration has brought to bear on the religious right's most recent attempt at integrating church and state. An excellent example of this sophistication can be seen in the criticisms that House Democrats and moderate Republicans raised early in Bush's term in their failed attempt to deny passage of legislation establishing the Office of Faith-Based Initiatives as a legal part of the federal government. They complained that religious organizations receiving government funding for welfare services would be exempt from complying with federal and state anti-discrimination laws as specified by Title VII of the 1964 Civil Rights Act, which forbids religious discrimination by employers. But Ashcroft's 1996 Charitable Choice legislation had already made religious institutions receiving public funding exempt from enforcing this aspect of federal labor law.

At the time that the Civil Rights Act was written, religious organizations were not receiving government subsidies for their activities. Now that their groups are being offered the opportunity to act as an arm of government, they have *carte blanche* to deny freedoms that the state has legally guaranteed all of its citizens employed with government funding since the mid-1960s. Thus, as Jake Tapper contended in a recent article in *Salon*, religious institutions like Bob Jones University, well-known for its ban on interracial dating amongst its student body, can, under the terms of this proposed legislation, forbid such race mixing—and still receive federal moneys for welfare services. Another example: In 1998, Louisville therapist Alice Pedreira, who worked at a Baptist-run facility for at-risk youth receiving nearly three quarters of its funding from the state of Kentucky to provide a variety of social services, was fired simply because, as her termination letter explained, Pedreira's "homosexual lifestyle is contrary to Kentucky Baptist Homes for Children['s] core values." The Bush Administration's advocacy of faith-based initiatives is a clear indication of conservatives' desire to get government out of the business of insuring the civil rights of all Americans.

The attempt to reintegrate church and state is, in fact, a cover for dismantling most of the social progress that was made during the twentieth century, from the mid-century establishment of the New Deal welfare state to the expansion of civil rights for minorities and women during the post–World War II period. Indeed, for the Bush administration, religion is synonymous with privatization and a white, heterosexual Protestant political hegemony.

What remains open to question is why on earth a pseudo-religious regime like this was ever allowed to assume power. Of course, it can be convincingly argued that Al Gore lost the presidential election because Bush senior's friends on the Supreme Court helped override a loss of the popular vote. But that would be making things too easy. A large percentage of Americans voted for our theocratic Dubya, and an even greater number take no issue with his fundamental religious message. Despite all of the technology, media resources, and education our nation possesses, most Americans see no major conflict between faith and democracy.

Much of the blame for the election results can be laid at the feet of the Democrats for failing to offer an inclusive secular alternative to the message of the Republicans. If anything, the Democrats can be criticized for giving faith too much credit. Mind you, I'm not suggesting that they should have concentrated on winning the atheist vote: Some studies show that ninety-two percent of all Americans believe in God, irrespective of political affiliation, and over forty percent attend church services on a regular basis. Rather, the so-called opposition party can be faulted for bolstering the impression that there is no dissent from the Republican conviction that Americans support the reintegration of church and state.

In particular, the responsibility for this strategic error can be placed on the Democrats' Jewish vice-presidential candidate, Joseph Lieberman, who actually spoke more about the role that faith should play in public life than Bush himself. As Lieberman put it, "We need to reaffirm our faith and renew the dedication of our nation and ourselves to God and God's purposes." This, from the most successful minority religious politician to date, not to mention a representative of a community that has fought ferocious battles to create a secular public sphere.

The evangelical community made itself strategically invisible during the election campaign to avoid compromising the prospects of a born-again fratboy aristocrat from Texas who was out to colonize the political center. Bush's most widely reported religious utterance came prior to the Iowa Caucus. When asked who his favorite political philosopher was, Bush responded, "Jesus Christ." Bush did speak of the role faith played in restoring his marriage, curing his alcoholism, and the like. But he never really connected this classic faith-as-therapy narrative to the religious program that he is now attempting to install in Washington.

Throughout the election, Bush remained in constant contact with leaders of the greater religious right, assembling what he called a Values Defense Team, including representatives of the Christian Coalition, the Southern Baptist Convention, and Jerry Falwell, whose voter registration campaign, People of Faith 2000, was tremendously effective in getting out the vote for Bush. Nearly all of Bush's religious supporters adhered to a highly disciplined, low-profile ethos. As Jerry Falwell told the *New York Times,* "We have a presidential candidate and we have a vice-presidential candidate, both of whom are pro-life, pro-family, and pro-strong national defense. Our crowd needs to get into the battle, keep their mouths shut, and help this man win." Sure enough, they did.

This all reads like a script from a movie about how a historically marginalized community eventually regained power. In this case, it becomes incumbent on those uncomfortable with the status quo to try to read the situation against the grain. What if, per chance, the potential reconciliation of church and state in America weren't so much about religion finally being integrated into public life as much as the government taking over the power of the church? This may seem a counter-intuitive assumption. After all, this is the era of globalization, in which entities like the nation-state are no longer supposed to be viable; multinational corporations and international trading bodies such as the WTO have increasingly assumed the powers that governments once exercised—regulating trade, formulating laws, redistributing wealth—while compelling elected officials to do their bidding.

If this globalization process really does represent the state of the world today, it would make sense for people to instinctively seek out icons of authority and power to protect themselves from the ruthless anarchy of a wholly privatized world. Ever since Karl Marx first labeled religion the opiate of the masses, many a progressive has sought to explain religion as *the* alienated symptom of working-class disenfranchisement in a tragically futile search for consolation.

But the historical circumstances surrounding Bush's attempt to bridge the gap between church and state force us to do more than once again call upon this classically reactionary reading of religion. These circumstances compel us to expand that reading to include the privileged as well as the poor. This standard leftist critique is only relevant when it comes to understanding the ideologies that mystify poverty, not the narcissistic mythologies invoked by anxiety-ridden governing elites to justify their own institutional legitimacy. Add to the equation the idea that globalization represents a diffusion of political power, in which the state has to share authority with the economy, and you get a crisis of competition in which every element of the worldwide establishment is jockeying for recognition of its own hegemony. Since the state can no longer assume its inherent superiority, it must disguise its growing impotence. That's the only way for it to compete effectively with the market forces trying to colonize the same mind-share.

Why not make the state's disempowerment seem natural by reconstructing it as a hybrid entity in which religion provides the only reasonable response to the market? In this scenario, the idea of freedom gets packaged to fit within the bounds of religion. Liberation is then only possible in the next life, when the state-as-church will be magically transformed into the church-as-state. When a judicially appointed president tells us that freedom flows through him from our Heavenly Father, it ought to make you suspicious. Anyone want to say, "Bait and switch?"

Clearly I'm not the world's most religious person. Even as a teenager, when I turned briefly to Buddhism, the nature of my spirituality was not particularly spiritual. I gravitated to Buddhism, in part, as a way of articulating my *political* opposition to a life circumscribed by religion—by my Jewish heritage on the one hand and my Christian milieu on the other. Buddhism gave me a way of saying, "I won't be tricked into believing what you want me to believe." In this respect, my behavior was analogous to that of the left-wing Muslims in India who became increasingly religious as a way of doing battle with a state that excluded them from the political process. But the comparison only goes so far, since I didn't even have roots in my religion of choice. In fact, I chose Buddhism precisely because it was the least like a proper religion.

But as I grew older, I began to realize that I would need to reconnect with the religion of my forebears. I didn't feel the desire to be born again as a Jew; rather, I wanted to consider my heritage critically. Over the years, my interest in religious studies narrowed in two directions. On the one hand, I began to research the religious right in the United States, the fruits of which you've tasted in the preceding pages. Simultaneously, I started to analyze my favorite leftist theorists through the filter of religion. Walter Benjamin, Theodor Adorno, Herbert Marcuse, and Karl Marx were all deeply skeptical about organized religion. Yet they also shared a Jewish heritage. The more I studied them, the more I found that, for all of their commitment to secular politics, their work reflected an approach to history conditioned by the experience of Jewishness. Indeed, they were able to critique capitalism so effectively by recognizing the afterimage of religion within it.

More recently, I've begun the process of actually coming to terms with my own past. Although I was born to a steadfastly secular family, I can see how thoroughly our secularism is imbued with religion. For Jewish families like my own, the religious impulse was long ago redirected toward the nation of Israel. The result is a startling paradox. Our religion is the state, even while we have done everything in our power to prevent the state from being reduced to a religion. Maybe this is why I'm so sensitive to the dangers of undermining the separation of church and state. In the religious politics of George W. Bush and his supporters, I see distorted reflections of my family's manufactured homeland. As I write, the supporters of secular politics in Israel are in a headlong retreat, pushed out of power by reactionaries intent on transforming the state *as* religion into an inflexible state *of* religion. The parallels to the United States are striking. It is a depressing prospect.

I have long had decidedly ambivalent feelings about my upbringing. I did not have an easy childhood, and my family's loyalty to the state of Israel was a primary factor. Nevertheless, as I look back on my heritage from a vantage point in the twenty-first century, I find myself confronting waves of nostalgia for a time when fighting for Israel meant something more than it does today. The desire to redeem my heritage began a few years back, when Israeli Premier Yitzhak Rabin was murdered by a right-wing fanatic, a man of his own people.

The morning after Rabin's assassination, I called my father in Tel Aviv to offer him my condolences. As usual, there was nary a sign of emotion in his voice. But this time the silence was overwhelming. Finally, I managed to goad Elie into speaking, and when he did, all the rage and sorrow of his long life rushed out. "These Jewish settlers are all brownshirts," he said, "just like the Irgun were before independence." To understand the severity of my father's words, one must be familiar with his particular generation of Israelis. Elie was born in British-occupied Palestine three years after the First World War, and worked as a shipping expert in charge of smuggling Jews out of liberated concentration camps at the end of the Second World War. Rabin's assassination must have been one of the most tragic moments in his life. As though this were the only time I felt I could establish a sense of shared conviction, I responded, "Now, Abba, do you see why my work on the religious right is justified?"

I have a very hard time separating religion from death because, like many Jews brought up in the shadow of the Holocaust, I was raised to believe that dodging death was an essential part of my ethnic identity; everything we did was in some way related to self-preservation. It wasn't just Elie's stories of seeing the open pits full of stinking, decrepit bodies, which I heard repeated over and over again as a child as though they were morally instructive mantras. It was largely my entire family's single-minded devotion to the state of Israel. Though we spent little time in the country, Israel was always with us. We were a classically politicized post-war countercultural Jewish family forging its own national identity as Israelis—as our own way of redressing the massive trauma that our people had experienced.

While it may be difficult to see the progressive political legitimacy of such a project today, during the late 1940s, when my father was deeply immersed in the effort to build the state of Israel as Chief of Ocean Transport for the Haganah (the military wing of the Yishuv, the provisional Jewish governing body of Palestine at the time), it was impossible to avoid a culture centered around the condemnation of murder. Israel, in short, became the expression of collective life instincts. Around this ethos, my family's identity and its political ideology were molded. Despite having spent most of my life in the Diaspora, I continue to instinctively check wire reports every time I hear about a suicide bombing, fearful that a relative might have been involved.

That's why, when well-meaning Christians and Orthodox Jews ask me how come I don't believe in God, I really don't know what to say except that for me religion is all about death. What more can I say? That fear is my God? Well, yes. In fact, fear is everything. With fear, you only have the present moment, in all of its intractably violent, atheistic glory. No matter how hard people may work to find space for the divine, their religious identity will inevitably be the sum total of a history of violence. I don't see how religion can be a matter of unquestioning allegiance to an abstract set of principles.

Defining it as blind faith is utterly foreign to me. Instead, I was given Middle-Eastern geography to round everything out.

I first began to deify Israel at the age of eight when my father took me to Masada after sprinkling the ashes of my dead mother from the door of a military helicopter at dawn. Masada was a mountaintop fortress to which the remnants of the last Jewish rebellion against the Roman Empire retreated in 73 A.D. in order to delay their inevitable defeat. After the defenders had been under siege for six months, Rome's Fifth Legion finally began to ascend this six-thousand-foot mountain overlooking the Dead Sea. When the fortress commanders realized they were going to be overtaken, they ordered the heads of each family to slit the necks of their wives and children. So when my father—the war hero—sprinkled my mother's ashes from the summit two thousand years later, his action was motivated by the burden of history, as though my mother were a victim of the same ancient struggles, and my father a modern-day Zealot who had sacrificed her for the sake of freedom.

However, that was 1975. A lot has changed since then. It would be impossible now to commit such a legitimately sentimental act without invoking the pathological breed of Israelis who invest *too much* meaning in the land—like the settlers and members of the national-religious camp. Just look at Rabin's assassin, Yigal Amir: He's the antithesis of everyone we knew in Israel in my early years. To be sure, my father's actions on Masada indulged in a highly politicized religious narrative. He was, in essence, declaring that my mother was a metaphorical casualty of the Jewish struggle for survival. Sadly, the difference between performing such a ritual twenty-five years ago and performing it now is that the Israel to which he dedicated his life has itself become a casualty of that same struggle.

Israel is also an older state than it was during the 1970s. It has developed and nurtured its own reactionary ideologies and shed its cloak of youthful innocence. Now, Israel is more than just a part of the Bible—it's also a part of the modern world. In nearly every town there's a branch of Tower Records. In nearly every hand there's a cellphone. And in nearly every home there's a computer with an Internet connection. Even so, none of this is synonymous with the *Wired*-style democratic modernity boosted by proponents of the new economy. They would have you believe that a decentralized, informed, fundamentally tolerant democracy is a necessary cultural corollary to the technologically advanced, "start-up" mentality of today's Israel. But they are wrong.

To the extent that Israel is still burdened with being Zion—the land that God gave to the Jews—it remains so with a vengeance. For all of its superficial transcendence of the backwardness and poverty that prevails elsewhere in the Middle East, contemporary Israel is the captive of a vigorously conservative religious community that bears little resemblance to the country's largely secular, socialist pioneers who dreamt of turning the barren sands of Tel Aviv, as Theodor Herzl once imagined in *Der Alte Neuland*, into the cobblestone streets of a new Vienna. Those pioneers built a country that is now characterized by its decaying bauhaus high-rises, colored black by air pollution, and filled with people who are bombarded with religious propaganda and American television programs. These angry people take their first extended vacation from home when they perform their military service in the Golan Heights, Gaza, or the West Bank. It's not a lifestyle conducive to breeding tolerance, no matter how many Blockbuster nights it makes possible. These angry people are the new Israelis. They represent an absurd kind of normalization, socialized in equal measure by a Euro-American consumer culture and more than half a century of continuous war and military occupation.

It all makes me wish things were the same as when I was a child. The roads weren't fully paved yet, and we could drive to

Nablus or Ramallah on a Saturday afternoon with the cartridge of my father's Kalashnikov assault rifle buried somewhere in the back of the car, and the gun's safety pin engaged. The older I get, the more my father's empty rifle comes to mind when I contemplate religion. That's not how I was instructed to conceive of spirituality as a teenager in America during the Reagan era. But for all the attempts at brainwashing I endured at the hands of my religious educators and through the American culture industry, that rifle has remained in my consciousness. It stands as a reminder of the price people pay for the freedom of religion. It also signals the particular sacrifices of *my* people: my ancestors, my relatives, my father. For all the burden of my personal history, however, I want to remember that gun as a weapon disarmed, an icon of a violent society rendered temporarily peaceful. I'm doing what I can to keep it in the back of my mind. And I'm doing what I can to keep it in the back of the car.

San Francisco, California, 2001

SEEING RED

One day last year, I was performing my morning ritual, listening to public radio as I cooked breakfast. *"London police prepare for May Day's anti-capitalism demonstrations,"* the BBC announced as its lead story. *"Thousands of demonstrators are planning to stop all business downtown to protest against capitalism."* I put down my coffee and stared at the radio in disbelief. What did she say? I asked myself. Anti-capitalism? I must be dreaming! Being a longtime Marxist, I couldn't help but grin with self-satisfaction. These words were candy in a mouth that had only ever tasted bitterness with politics. Hearing the report rendered so neutrally on a public news program felt like a huge victory.

As it turns out, of course, nothing much did come of it. Not yet, at least. I'm writing this in the fearsome first twelve months of George W. Bush's administration. Each day brings more bad news, layoffs, and bankruptcies in the high-tech industries of the San Francisco Bay Area, as well as new schemes to roll back environmental and civil-rights legislation. The impending new dawn I sensed that hopeful spring morning in 2000 has been eclipsed by the imposing bulk of neo-Reaganism. This unpleasant reality forces me to interrogate that brief window of optimism. Was I just deluding myself, like those music fans who saw the rock band Nirvana as the leading edge of a cultural revolution? Or were the seeds of a stronger, better left really being sown, regardless of the depressing outcome of Election 2000?

Beginning with the demonstrations that rocked the World Trade Organization meeting in Seattle in November 1999, more and more people started talking about the evils of globalization, about monopolization in the mass media, about the systemic problems confronting all of us. From the thousands of people who sought to reprise the "Battle of Seattle" at the IMF meeting in Washington, DC in April 2000; to the May Day 2000 anti-capitalism protestors who brought London to a standstill; to the struggles in the streets of Quebec City in 2001; to the recurring interviews on National Public Radio with figures like *No Logo* author Naomi Klein, patron saint of the anti-brand-name movement, and *Baffler* editor Tom Frank, critic of laissez-faire economics—the status quo was coming under attack with a force unmatched since the 1960s. And, for once, it wasn't just the intellectuals and "fringe types" employing words like "alienation" and "exploitation." Some mainstream news commentators even applauded the potential breakup of Microsoft. Anti-sweatshop activists picketing in front of The Gap and Old Navy stores actually seemed to be getting through to consumers.

None of this prepared me, however, for the media spectacle that developed around the demonstrations against the G-8 meeting in Genoa in July 2001. The protests were hotly anticipated by American and British newspapers. These same venues then gave ample coverage to the publication of *Empire*, a massive treatise on the possibilities for revolutionary transformation during the era of globalization, written by a jailed Italian Marxist philosopher,

Antonio Negri, and an American academic, Michael Hardt. The book was described by the Slovenian radical philosopher Slavoj Zizek as "the *Communist Manifesto* for our time," and the *New York Times* printed an op-ed piece by Negri and Hardt the day the G-8 summit began, a remarkable indication of their argument's burgeoning mainstream legitimacy. Not only was the movement that took flight in Seattle gaining momentum, it was also developing an identifiable, global intellectual base no longer derided for its classically Marxist anti-market positions.

As saddened as I was by the Italian Carabinieri's killing of Genoa protestor Carlo Giuliani, I was startled to read a report that his father was a longtime union organizer who identified with the older Italian left. Putting down the paper, I was as overwhelmed by the sense of historical continuity that this portrait of Giuliani's political heritage conveyed as I was by yet another mass demonstration against an emerging, decidedly undemocratic transnational political order. With estimates of more than 100,000 people in attendance, this unprecedented outpouring of discontent dwarfed the numbers involved in the Seattle demonstrations. While I still wasn't sure if these activists were entirely certain of their own agenda, the international makeup of the gathering was impossible to ignore.

For someone who feels that the sixties revolt has become too much of a fetish—that its repetitively invoked memories have constrained a newer left from forging its own unique historical identity—the tragedy of Giuliani's death was a bittersweet pedagogical victory. This instructive misfortune could not have come at a more symbolic time in the development of the post–Cold War left. Nor, for that matter, could it have happened in a more historically poignant location. Genoa is a city with a rich history of progressive politics, and was the only Italian city liberated by local partisans without the support of Allied forces during the

Second World War. This legacy is not lost on local politicians. Genoa, as city counselor Giancarlo Bonifai said in a recent interview with the BBC, has always been a site of mass movements, "like the worker movement and the student movement—dating back to when the [Italian] Socialist Party was founded in Genoa." In fact, the city named one of the primary thoroughfares in the port area—or, to be more precise, in the fenced off "red zone" where demonstrators were not permitted entry—after Antonio Gramsci, founder of the Italian Communist Party.

I have tried to put some critical distance between myself and these hopeful portents. Yet even as I do this, I am blinded by the silver lining. If these events aren't just a figment of my starry-eyed imagination, they pose profound questions about the precariousness of our transnational social order. It is hard not to feel like a cheerleader at a Communist Party meeting. Are we witnessing a resurgence of leftist politics? And, if so, why *now* rather than when we elected Ronald Reagan president, fought the Gulf War, or watched President Clinton eviscerate federal welfare programs?

The Cold War is ten years behind us, and enough time has passed to allow radical politics to be retooled for an age in which the specter of communism no longer worries people in the so-called free world. With the propagandistic rhetoric of the Eastern Bloc left for the history books, it is again possible to speak of capitalism without seeming like pawns of some totalitarian regime. Regardless of the precise political orientations—black, green, or red—of the new progressive movements that flexed their muscles on the streets of Seattle, London, Washington, DC, Quebec City, Gothenburg, and Genoa, consciousness of the destructive nature of capitalism constitutes the radical bottom line.

Like many progressives, I worry about the long-term impact that the attacks on the World Trade Center and the Pentagon will have on this new progressivism. With the US Department of Justice proposing draconian legislation that would permit wiretapping without judicial review, searches without warrants, and the seizure of business, banking, and academic records without establishing probable cause, the prospects for further Seattle-style mobilizations are bleak. After the destruction of one of the most prominent symbols of American global economic hegemony, the public will be susceptible to associating anti-market sentiment with terrorist activity. It may become very difficult to espouse economically progressive beliefs without being seen as ideologically complicit with mass-murderers.

Undoubtedly, these ramifications will be felt outside of the United States as well. Within two weeks of the attacks, for example, Italian security forces staged a massive crackdown on anti-capitalist organizations associated with the G-8 demonstrations in Genoa. Throughout the country, police raided squats and the offices of activist organizations, carting off computers, flyers, and photographs, and arresting anarchists under emergency anti-terrorism laws reminiscent of the grim days of the 1970s. Indeed, at a recent meeting in Berlin with German Chancellor Gerhard Shroeder and Russian President Vladimir Putin, Italian Prime Minister Silvio Berlusconi made the connection explicit. The *International Herald Tribune* quoted Berlusconi as stating that he saw "a singular coincidence between [the WTC/Pentagon attacks] and the anti-globalization movement."

Nevertheless, an awareness of the Cold War's diminishing power has made me ponder my own political education. Over the years, I've thought long and hard about where my intimacy with the left began. While I could cite many instances, I think the most revealing is the period of my childhood that I spent in Italy. After my mother's death in 1975, my father and I traveled to Genoa to close his office and move back home to Israel. Every morning we'd leave the albergo where we were staying, buy a copy of Italy's biggest daily, *Corriere Della Sera,* and head off to a café to drink tea and eat croissants on our dwindling savings. Though Elie was not exactly fluent in Italian, after nearly twenty years of working in the country, his knowledge of the language was strong enough to get him through a newspaper. Afflicted by a severe case of dyslexia, I still did not know how to read very well, so Elie would sit there every morning and translate articles for me, reading aloud in his neo-Victorian British military English.

Judging from what Elie first translated for me, what particularly concerned him were party politics. Granted, there was very little else to read about in Italian papers at the time. 1975 was the high point for Italian leftist terrorist groups like the Brigada Rossa. Bombs were exploding and politicians were getting kidnapped. Elie would routinely read me articles about these events, taking the time to answer my questions about the differences between Maoists and Marxists and about why there were both communist and socialist parties in the Italian parliament. He would smile and laugh at my difficulty in distinguishing between leftist factions, seeing in my naïveté certain kinds of truths in which older people would be loathe to indulge. "The only difference between them is which Mafia clan each of these parties comes from, Yoel. That's the only thing you need to remember."

After three months of performing this daily ritual, my father became more and more distracted, choosing to put his paper aside and write out telexes at breakfast. Having nothing to do except eat my croissants and stare out the window at the passing pedestrians and mopeds, I started trying to read the newspaper myself. I could barely read anything in English, let alone Italian. One morning I picked up a copy of *Corriere Della Sera* and found a picture on the front page of a suspicious-looking, unattractive man sporting a grown-out pompadour, with huge headlines surrounding his face in bold, black letters. The image was uncomfortable to look at, and I asked my father who the man was.

Elie set down his work, took the paper aside, adjusted his Henry Kissinger–like glasses, and replied, "That's Enrico Berlinguer, the head of the Italian Communist Party."

I couldn't have chosen a more appropriate communist icon to be frightened by, and buried in my infantile physical repulsion by Berlinguer's image was a seed of my lifelong inability to identify with the establishment left. A wealthy Sardinian from a fairly devout Catholic family, Enrico Berlinguer had finessed "The Great Compromise"—two years before that fall morning in Genoa, as chairman of the PCI—whereby the Communists joined the government for the first time, in coalition with their arch rivals, the Christian Democrats. Though they were not given any ministerial positions, the Communists in return promised to respect the law, cease its animosity toward the Church, back Italy's membership in NATO, fight left-wing terrorism, and help reinvigorate the Italian economy.

Of course, Berlinguer and the Communists also sought concessions, such as legalizing abortion, restructuring Italy's byzantine health-care system, strengthening regional governments, closing lunatic asylums, and deregulating the broadcasting industry. In this regard, Berlinguer's alliance with the Christian Democrats increased the respectability of the Communists amongst Italy's middle class, whose voter approval pushed the PCI within two percentage points of the Christian Democrats in Italy's general elections in June 1975. But it also set the stage for dragging the left into Italy's notoriously corrupt, paternalistic political culture.

In retrospect, this fusion was an important precedent for the "Third Way" socialists who governed Italy in the second half of the 1990s under the guise of the "Olive Tree" coalition. Ironically, to bring public spending within the limits specified by the European Union, the coalition, led by a reconstituted PCI (now called the PDS, or Party of the Democratic Left), was entrusted with dismantling Italy's welfare state by cutting pensions and privatizing state holdings like the public telecommunications franchise. By the spring of 2001, with the Italian economy performing poorly and crime levels at an all-time high in northern cities—compounded by heightened public concern about illegal immigration from Albania and Africa—arch-conservative Fininvest media magnate Silvio Berlusconi and his Forza Italia party were finally able to put Berlinguer's progeny out to pasture. In his second successful bid for the prime minister's office, Berlusconi assembled a powerful coalition of right-wing parties, including the separatist Northern League, led by Umberto Bossi, and the neo-fascist National Alliance, headed up by aging Mussolini acolyte, Gianfranco Fini.

The transformation of the Italian left over the past quarter-century feels like a confirmation of my childish reaction to Berlinguer's image in the newspaper. For months afterwards I fixated upon the photo, repeatedly asking myself, *Is that what all communists look like?* I worried that if I ever became a communist, I'd have to become Italian and look like Berlinguer. From that point on, newspapers and communism became inseparable for me. In essence, communism thus became my entry into the worlds of both literacy and politics.

To this day, the word "communism" retains a special power over me. In early August 1999, several weeks after NATO ended its aerial bombardment of the former Yugoslavia, I picked up copies of the Sunday *New York Times* and the *San Francisco Chronicle* and counted the word at least nine times. Not surprisingly, it was used in each case to illustrate how much better things are now that the Soviet Union is defunct. Curiously enough, a couple of articles went so far as to compare the superiority of everyday life in capitalist countries to the conditions that prevail under communist circumstances *in the present tense*—and they weren't writing about Cuba. Some of the writers expressed such a strong sense of ongoing conflict that it seemed as though the Cold War were still in progress.

When I took notice of this, I asked myself whether these journalists really knew what they were talking about, or whether they were living out some kind of masochistic fantasy about what it must have been like to live in an authentic totalitarian society. My immediate assumption was that their active obsession with communism was symptomatic of the aftereffects of decades of wartime propaganda. Never having witnessed the real thing, but having been radically indoctrinated by forty years of Cold-War ideology, they had instinctively forced themselves to live out what it must have been like to exist on the other side of the fence.

But then something strange occurred to me. What if these hyperbolic cranks, despite their obvious gloating, were working to keep something alive by continuously invoking its passing? Remembrance has a funny way of doing that. It seems that the rhetoric of anti-communism has been absorbed so thoroughly into our psyches that we still can't think about politics without it—even if, like most Americans, we only experienced communism as a fictional construct delivered by the mass media. The compulsion to remind ourselves of something we never had the misfortune to experience becomes an experience in its own right.

No matter how forward-thinking we imagine ourselves to be, the afterimage of communism still obscures our vision of the future. This strange circumstance testifies to our inability to cope with a world in which there are fewer and fewer pockets of difference. As I write this in late 2001, America closely resembles the "one dimensional society" that Herbert Marcuse described in 1964 in trying to spell out the politics of the coming service economy. The dystopia he envisioned would be marked by a total loss of historical memory of revolutionary alternatives to the established order. It would be a society in which an "unhappy consciousness" would use the ruse of free expression to direct our dissatisfaction with the present into productive economic behavior. Instead of making us "repressed" like our nineteenth-century forebears, this new order would permit us everything—except the opportunity to overturn it. Where our predecessors had learned to sublimate their sexual urges in order to be productive, we would become productive by indulging them. Marcuse's account of "repressive desublimation" reveals the lie at the heart of our "free" society.

Part of what makes our illusion of freedom so pernicious is that we have become incapable of making the moral distinctions between "us" and "them" that motivated activists during the sixties. Marcuse was actually describing the unhappy consciousness of the *left*. If reification involves a kind of forgetting, then the aging sixties left is certainly guilty of succumbing to its effects. As popular histories of the achievements of that period suggest, the left failed to foresee certain developments—such as the backlash against the "excesses" of the counterculture—that would pave the way for the conservative politics of the present day.

Ignoring a steady stream of right-wing political achievements, many leftists still place a great deal of stock in the notion that American politics remain dominated by a mythic political center. As they see it, some folks swing to the right of center, others swing to the left, but no one ever moves very far away from the middle, unless they are what newspapers and politicians are fond of calling "hardliners" or "extremists." This perception belies a failure to see beneath the surface of democratic rhetoric. Most Americans, with the exception of ultra-right-wingers, shy away from being labeled as zealots of any political persuasion. The language with which Americans have learned to talk politics—best characterized by the concept of *inclusivity*, as discussed in the first section of this book—almost always implies liberal political commitments, even when the ideas expressed are highly conservative. In this context, using language that overtly affirms one's political identity tends to be too *exclusive*, and therefore unacceptable. Does this mean that most Americans really can be defined as "middle of the road"? Not at all. As we have seen with the radical right, there is substantial resistance to the state in places where the vast majority of leftists fear to tread. And most of the people dreaming of a *coup d'état* aren't sitting at home in a Rage Against the Machine T-shirt reading Che Guevara's *Motorcyle Diaries*. More likely, they can be found playing paintball, barbecuing on the infield of Charlotte Motor Speedway, or, dare I say it, praying in a house of worship.

Leftists, unfortunately, have a hard time overcoming their investment in the rhetoric of democratic inclusiveness. To be sure, if you say you're a leftist, plenty of Americans will think that you are ignoring the fall of the Berlin Wall. And if you say you're a right-winger, people assume that you're a racist who wants to bring back segregation. But you can always express your opinions in popular code, paying lip service to the rules governing political expression. These rules have been shaped by the now-discredited liberal political ideologies which label right-wing discourse "hate speech" (when it deals with matters of race) and left-wing discourse "hard-line" (when it deals with matters of class). You can call for revolution, but it's got to be cultural, not political. You can criticize capitalism, but it's got to be based on a preference for small businesses over multinational corporations. And you can voice hatred of women, Jews, homosexuals, and ethnic minorities, but you have to use language that reflects how minorities infringe upon your own *right* to discriminate in a democratic society.

Right-wing demagogues are far more proficient at this double-speak than their counterparts on the left. For example, an evangelical Christian might say, "My right to worship Jesus Christ is demeaned when other religions have the same right to worship their own gods." A libertarian could argue that "all forms of state intervention in the economy are undemocratic because they restrict the basic rights of producers to create commodities." Or a white supremacist could say, "Giving blacks and Hispanics the same rights as whites discriminates against whites' right to live in a white society." What we find here is a distinction between rhetoric and meaning, with Americans employing language informed by liberalism in order to communicate conservative political sentiments. What's most troubling is how effectively conservatives have learned to navigate through the liberal rules governing linguistic conduct. Once you learn the language of rights, you can use it to argue on behalf of anything.

Right-wing political discourse is, in fact, paradigmatic of the manner in which Americans communicate their political identities. Conversely, few leftists have a clear sense of the message they wish to communicate in code. They tend to speak in the code our society demands but have lost the key needed to decipher the words in leftist terms. Frequently, the rhetoric of democracy is all they have left. It's a curious situation, but one that goes a long way toward explaining the impoverishment of contemporary progressivism. Indeed, one could argue that it has been so long since leftists learned to speak in liberal code that they've become indistinguishable from neo-conservatives. The left doesn't communicate radically anti-democratic ideas clothed in liberal rhetoric; instead, it communicates cultural ideas that are largely neo-conservative.

For instance, during the debate in California over affirmative action in the late 1990s, many opponents of the proposed legislation (to essentially roll back gains made in the sixties and seventies) appealed to California's tradition of cultural and institutional respect for civil rights and equal opportunities for minorities. Since when do leftists call for reliance on *traditions* of civic tolerance? "Tradition" used to be a bad word on the left because it connoted a fearful and unconscious attachment to convention and procedure. This is a far cry from the anti-establishment fantasy once espoused by the New Left.

Another obvious example of this trend is when liberal political activists complain about multinational corporations ruining traditional, indigenous ways of life—implying that foreigners would be better off if we let them remain close to nature, without toilets, air conditioning, or roads to drive on. Such activists harp on the introduction of television and decadent western customs, the end of neo-feudal hunter-gatherer societies, and the decline of ancient wisdom cultures as a way of criticizing American economic imperialism. Though excited by the anti-capitalism demonstrations of the past several years, I have also found myself recoiling at the number of participants acting on neo-tribalist beliefs. By contrast, the New England Puritans of the 1600s would have seemed genuinely progressive.

Many leftists use language and concepts that equate traditional, pre-modern ways of life with wholeness in the same manner as conservatives. Furthermore, anti-capitalism is by no means the sole domain of the left. As addressed earlier, the right is at times equally critical of the effects that modern society has on conventional ways of life. Examining the language Americans employ, then, we get a sense of the overwhelming hegemony of conservative ideology on all sides of the political spectrum. We also attain a greater awareness of the transitional historical moment we're living in, with few remaining distinctions between left and right—mostly just different gradations of similar conservative sentiments. Some are more extreme than others, but many are unified by a resistance to change.

Under the influence of such seminal conservative (and Nazi-friendly) political thinkers as Friedrich Nietzsche and Martin Heidegger, many scholars and social commentators on the right as well as the post-socialist left—e.g., Michel Foucault, Jean-François Lyotard—have argued that we are living in an essentially post-political age. They say it has become impossible to make distinctions between right and left because politics are all about false consciousness. One way for leftists to crudely interpret this is that political ideologies have been replaced by the free market. Attempts to map out alternative political orientations are considered delusional, because politics, like religion, harken back to a time of meta-narratives which no longer hold sway in the disenchanted world of pure capital—where even the state is now just another impotent, yet comforting construct.

If modern capitalism demythologized religion, it also demythologized politics, which is why no lasting alternatives to capitalism emerged in the twentieth century that weren't totalitarian. It appears foolish to indulge in utopian political ideologies: No matter how humanitarian they try to be, they always devolve into their inhumane doubles—as Marxism did in becoming Stalinism. Now that the Cold War is over and even the mighty Russian bear drinks Coca Cola and runs on Microsoft Office, we are more sure of this than ever. This is what it means to live a late phase of capitalist demythologization. As Cyndi Lauper once put it, money changes everything. Marx would surely have agreed with her. According to this type of postmodern logic, the best alternative to capitalism at our disposal is to develop post-political alternatives for creating a more just society, such as forcing what's left of the state to legitimate ethnic, sexual, and cultural difference—because it wouldn't make economic sense not to. This brings us back to the boycott of Disney. Is our only "political" alternative the purchase of *Lion King* paraphernalia?

All that prejudice and discrimination against minorities

amounts to is an exercise in economic irrationality, guided by outmoded racist ideologies corresponding to previous, less evolved stages in capitalist development. As the economy continues its inexorable expansion, every difference becomes a potential market signifier. Queers have a lot of buying power, Jews are good financial planners, women make better homes than men, and aborted children aren't dependent on free school lunches. Everyone serves a purpose in the new holy order. The problem with this kind of anti-political ideology is that it's too cynical and accommodating to function as a political philosophy. But that's precisely the point: Philosophical anti-politics, in whatever guise, cultural or academic, are a product of deep disappointment not only with the left's failures to combat the right, but more importantly, with the contemporary left's own conservatism.

While academic leftists familiar with the history of European socialist politics would naturally like to think that the anti-politics of French postmodernism were an alienated response to the reactionary politics of the French Communist Party (current party chief Robert Hue is alleged to have not even begun to acknowledge Stalin's crimes until the mid-seventies), there are better explanations for the left's failures. The real dilemma lies with the political nature of free-market economic systems, and the fact that they are neither entirely conservative nor entirely progressive. As any economist will tell you, capitalist modes of production are revolutionary because they have to consistently reinvent themselves in order to keep producing new commodities. At the same time, however, capitalism also relies on conservatism to survive.

Nonetheless, the left doesn't seem to grasp that conservative culture is not the equivalent of the capitalist production process. The right will at times react negatively to the trauma that accompanies changes in capitalist development, such as downsizing, outsourcing, or the replacement of industrial economies with service economies; but cultural conservatism always returns in the end to legitimate these very sources of economic modernization. Since the sixties, the left has been particularly out-of-sync with changes in capitalist development, and the language it employs has not been updated to accommodate the decline of industrial production in first world countries. But the language of the right has. This is why American conservatives are now talking about their right to renounce rights altogether. They've updated their political culture to acknowledge the passing of Fordism. The American left has not, which is why it can't seem to identify its own enemies, and sounds, for the moment, a lot more conservative than the right.

Sorting out the complexities of political language has never been so difficult. Leftists are caught between a rock and a hard place. The passing of the Cold War has made the revolutionary rhetoric of the left seem distant, dated, maybe even dead. Fearing that they will be ignored by mainstream society, some leftists have opted to use the centrist language popularized by neo-liberal politicians like Bill Clinton and Tony Blair. (Blair laughed at former Italian Prime Minister Massimo D'Alema when he invoked the word "socialism" at a gathering of "Third Way" leaders in Europe several years ago.) At the same time, the rhetoric of revolution has been mined by advertising copywriters and conservatives alike. In order to critique contemporary capitalism, leftists resort to words like "values" and "traditions" that can't easily be incorporated into a meaningful leftist political program. Right-wingers, by contrast, speak confidently of "progress" and "revolution," even as they seek to perpetuate the injustices of the present social order. Truly, the political world has gone topsy-turvy.

So what am I suggesting? That leftists should once again strike the revolutionary pose of a Che Guevara? That they should proudly declare themselves to be communists in spite of everything that word now implies? Or that leftists should, rather, learn from right-wing political demagogues how to advance radical political goals from within a superficially liberal framework? Individually, none of these measures seems particularly attractive. Taken together, however, they might add up to something. But the real answer, I think, is to pay closer attention to the role of history in the present, gaining awareness of our conditioning as we navigate the ironies of contemporary existence. At the very least, this approach should open our eyes to some of the details that neo-liberalism renders invisible. Sometimes, the devil is in a *lack* of detail, as the recent history of the former Yugoslavia makes painfully clear.

The American government announced during the fall of 1998 that it was threatening military intervention in the Yugoslav province of Kosovo, where an ethnic Albanian guerilla movement seeking independence from Serbia had been fighting since early spring. Initially, rebel forces had made surprising advances, seizing over half of the territory from ill-prepared Serbian troops. But the Yugoslav army counterattacked, rolling back rebel gains with alarming intensity. Towns and villages were being razed to the ground. Several hundred thousand refugees were forced to leave their homes after being targeted by heavy artillery. Civilians were getting slaughtered. It seemed like the events of the early nineties were being repeated. The only difference was that this was Kosovo, not Croatia.

America wasn't eager to get directly involved in the fighting. It already had its hands full in Bosnia, where NATO had been put in charge of rebuilding the country as part of the diplomatic settlement reached in Dayton, Ohio in 1995. At the time that America began threatening Belgrade with intervention, elections were underway in Bosnia to constitute a multi-ethnic government under UN supervision. The last thing that NATO wanted was to destabilize its own three-year-old effort to rebuild the ex-Yugoslav republic with yet another war that would re-ignite tensions between Christians and Muslims. The straw that broke the camel's back was startling evidence of a renewed campaign of "ethnic cleansing" in Kosovo. Twenty-one members of a Muslim Albanian clan in the town of Rajac were found horribly mutilated in the woods not far from their family compound. Unwilling to once again take the blame for a failure to prevent genocide, NATO warned that it would attack and prepared its forces to strike Serbia. This won a temporary cease-fire agreement between the warring Yugoslav factions.

According to the terms of the ceasefire, federal troops and police forces deployed in Kosovo would be withdrawn, and negotiations granting the primarily Muslim province political autonomy would begin. The idea, as US diplomats explained, was to restore the region to its Tito-era status as a full province, which had been revoked by former Prime Minister Slobodan Milosevic in 1988, sparking not only the Kosovo independence movement but also the gradual disintegration of the former Yugoslavia. Under the threat of massive NATO air strikes, Serbia reluctantly agreed to go along, as did representatives from Kosovo's fledgling independence movement who saw it as an opportunity to regroup for the next stage of the conflict.

It didn't take long for the cease-fire to break down. Kosovo Liberation Army forces moved into territory vacated by government troops and attacked the Serbian military again. While attempting to give the appearance of respecting the terms of the cease-fire agreement, the Yugoslav government staged mass arrests of Muslims suspected of collusion with the rebels, and continued to routinely shoot civilians on counterinsurgency missions. Despite the fact that the crisis had temporarily fallen from the front pages of newspapers filled with Clinton scandal, Kosovo seemed like it might erupt at any moment.

I anxiously followed this display of violent political theater. Nothing in recent years had thrust me more into a political crisis than the civil war in the former Yugoslavia in the early nineties. I shared in the sense of crisis that the war instilled in the post–Cold War left, because I understood what a precious exception to the Stalinist rule Yugoslavia had become during the East-West conflict. Combining a large welfare state with a mixed economy and an official policy of multiculturalism that reconciled, however uneasily, Yugoslavia's many ethnicities and religions in a socialist melting pot, Tito's FRY promised to become an example of real political Enlightenment that Western social democracies could truly envy. And, as a Jew, I cautiously identified with the religious subtext to the conflict—much of it seemed to be a replay of traditionally Christian genocidal impulses toward non-Christian European citizens. Now that Eastern Europe's Jews were gone, who better to turn on than Muslims, a cultural minority demonized as the Western world's new enemy?

Part of me had wanted very desperately for the Americans to intervene and save Bosnia's Muslim population precisely because I still naïvely hoped that something had been learned from our failure to prevent the Holocaust. But I was also reluctant to see America move into such a position, as time and time again, from the Second World War to the Gulf War, America has only deployed its forces abroad to serve its own geo-economic interests. As much as I wanted some knight in shining democratic armor to save the day, I could find no obvious alternatives to the status quo. Anyone who'd intervene on behalf of Bosnia's Muslims would do so with another pretext in mind. This was not pure enough for me, because there had to be, to put it bluntly, *a final solution*. Anything else would simply be repugnant. But I knew this wouldn't happen, so I resigned myself to trying to decipher what it was that upset me most about the conflict.

In the end, I found myself wondering why history always seems to repeat itself. Somehow, if I could break that problem open, I might be able to see out to the other side and get a sense of legitimate alternatives to powerlessness and shame. By 1998, watching the Serbs inaugurate yet another chapter of ethnic cleansing against Yugoslavia's last substantial Muslim population, I was no longer searching my soul the way I had during the war in Bosnia. But the new war *did* prompt me to recall how I had found a better way to deal with such vexing moral problems—rather than attempt to explain them away like my activist and academic friends—and still retain some sense of humanity in the process.

It was July 1995, and I had been working as a part-time ship manager in the south of Spain for almost two months. Every time I went into town to buy groceries, I'd end up sitting through massive traffic jams. Although I worked with Americans and Englishmen, and despite the fact that we were in Spain, we stuck to a traditional North American nine-to-five work schedule. While we were leaving work at five, everyone else was headed back to work following their afternoon *siesta*.

This time I decided to try something different. I left the dock at three, expecting to cruise down the road unimpeded. No such luck. I got stuck as soon as I drove my beat-up little Renault onto the highway. But the congestion was coming from a different source. When I looked out at the traffic descending the hill beneath me, I saw a line of olive-green military trucks filled with ammunition, troops, and .50 caliber Browning machine gun barrels poking out from underneath camouflage tarps.

What the hell is going on? I thought to myself, as a pair of charcoal-gray and black United States Air Force F-16s buzzed over the ocean to my right. I knew from my Israeli upbringing that it was rare for military convoys to use civilian roads unless there was some kind of large-scale mobilization under way. Once I arrived in the neighboring town of Almuñecar, I called the captain that we'd recently hired and told him what I had seen. "Oh, that makes sense," he said. "There's been all this military transport chatter on marine radio today. It sounds like NATO is finally getting ready to ship out to Bosnia."

A week later, my girlfriend Cristina and I set out to Paris for a quick vacation. After crossing through French border control, we headed north for Lyon. Unlike the Spanish coastal highway, this road seemed relatively empty. But then we noticed the traffic heading in the opposite direction. Hundreds of camouflaged French armored personnel carriers full of troops wearing combat-ready flack jackets were traveling south, apparently en route to the port of Marseille. They were followed by huge trailer trucks carrying Leclerc battle tanks, each sporting 120mm guns tied down to their chassis, with French military symbols on their turrets instead of standard UN peacekeeping insignia. The absence of United Nations emblems meant this was a full-fledged combat deployment. Preparations for war had obviously begun. Armored cars would have been one thing, but heavy battlefield weapons like these suggested something entirely different.

The last time I had been in Paris, the war in Bosnia was just beginning to heat up. I remember eating dinner at my elder cousin Francis's suburban home in Ozoir, watching French television repeatedly show footage of the blown-apart bodies of dead shoppers in an open-air market in Sarajevo that had been bombed by the Serbs. All my elderly relatives could do was talk about the Nazis, how they'd returned to Europe in the form of the Serbian army. It was difficult for me to stomach such comparisons: people of all political and ethnic stripes—Jews, right-wingers, and leftists alike—still use the designation of "Nazi" to describe anything that remotely resembles racism. I argued with my cousins about it at great length, insisting that nationalism was being invoked in the place of communism to compensate for the crisis brought on by the collapse of state socialism in Eastern Europe.

"As much as leftists might not want to believe it," I said to Francis, "fascism was linked to socialism. This is entirely different."

"Yes, I agree, Joel," he replied. "But the genocide against the Muslims is the first time we've experienced anything like the Shoah in Europe since the war. So these comparisons, regardless of your scholarly hair-splitting, are entirely reasonable. Especially coming from the mouths of French Jews like us, who narrowly escaped the gas chambers."

I recalled how many Americans were voicing the same opinion when the first reports of "ethnic cleansing" started to surface in American newspapers in 1992—after the Yugoslav Federation had disintegrated and Serbia and Croatia began to carve up the weakest republic, Bosnia-Herzegovina. Around that time, reports had started to filter in about the existence of Serbian and Croatian concentration camps like Omarska, where Muslim civilians were being starved to death; of pitched battles in major cities like Vukovar, where the entire focus was the elimination of the Croat civilian population; and of soldiers on every side brutally raping female prisoners to torment their enemies.

Every politician, statesman, journalist, and scholar who wrote about the conflict was absolutely incredulous about the new lack of civility in the western world. "How could this be happening again in modern Europe?" they asked. It seemed like the clock had been turned back to 1939. Regardless of which political system had given birth to it, state-sanctioned racism and genocide were back.

Exhausted from the previous day's twelve-hour drive, Cristina and I drank pot after pot of coffee in the motel dining room while we tried to read *Libération,* the daily leftist newspaper. We pulled apart hot croissants with our fingers, sipped fresh orange juice, softly kissed each other, and savored the idea that we were in France and in love. We had money in our pockets and only bookstores and museums to visit for four whole days. Then the bartender turned on a wide-screen television that spanned the length of the wall in front of us. On came *Pas de Comment*, a silent documentary news program.

The UN had just discovered mass graves containing thousands of Bosnian Muslim civilians buried after the town of Srebenica had been overrun by Serb forces. Their mangled, bullet-ridden bodies were still fresh; the blood on their clothing hadn't even dried. The camera silently followed the trail of corpses through each hastily dug grave, moving in closely to capture all the gory, beheaded details, then withdrew to show the faces of the disgusted Dutch peacekeeping force who had been allowed into the area to inspect the bodies.

I felt terribly queasy. It wasn't just the brutal garishness of the program that upset me. It was how the graphic, silent documentation of violence made me feel about myself at the time. Here I was, a middle-class graduate student on vacation in Paris with his fashionably bald québécois girlfriend, in an affluent European city engaging in extremely refined cultural activities—eating pastries, buying books, wandering through museums. I don't think I have ever felt more full of self-loathing than I did that first morning of my French vacation. In a human sense, my cousin Francis was right: Violence is violence, regardless of where it comes from. Being old enough to bear witness to genocide twice in his lifetime was the only justification he needed to connect the historical dots between Nazism and Serbian nationalism. I looked into my café au lait as it grew cold, contemplating how my commitment to studying critical theory made it nearly impossible for me to take things at face value, even when the horrifying evidence of history repeating itself was staring me in the face. I stood and left the table.

After packing our bags, Cristina and I got back on the road and drove to the Latin Quarter. We had no idea where we were going to stay that night so we parked near the University of Paris Sorbonne campus with the hope of finding a cheap bed-and-breakfast. Everywhere we turned, we saw flyers advertising meeting of academics and cultural action committees formed around the war in Bosnia. Some gatherings were scheduled to discuss the sexual character of the war (one flyer announced the formation of a committee to discuss the metapolitics of mass rape); other bulletins called for public discussion of Europe's responsibility to intervene in the conflict and put an end to the violence.

The odd-notice-out was a prominently displayed placard advertising a public meeting hosted by the Spartacist League. I was floored. It was a call for the working class to defend the socialist government of Yugoslav Prime Minister Slobodan Milosevic against Western imperialist attempts to derail his attack on Islamic fundamentalist encroachment in the Balkans. The poster urged the international working class to volunteer in the struggle against the rising green tide of European Islam. It was sickening how one-dimensional the plea was. But it struck me how much this opinion reflected the way I imagined many European leaders truly felt about the lessons that Balkan nationalism were teaching Europe's burgeoning Islamic community. The primary lesson seemed to be: Don't develop political aspirations or you'll be really fucking sorry.

It made sense. Anti-Islamic violence throughout France was on the rise. Supporters of National Front leader Jean-Marie Le Pen had murdered a North African immigrant several weeks before at a rally celebrating the party's electoral advances. The

French government had recently enacted a policy forbidding devout Muslim women from wearing their *chadors* (ritual headscarves) in public schools. The German government was resisting the granting of citizenship to German-born Turkish Muslim children of first-generation guest workers, while neo-Nazi activists were assaulting German Muslims under the pretense of combating Islamic fundamentalism. The French Spartacist posters pasted on the walls of Paris that day basically argued the same thing: *Stop Muslim growth in Europe.*

As much as I understood the anti-clerical subtext of this racist leftist poster—an overriding orthodox Marxist discomfort with all forms of religion—I was again outraged by how shallow the analysis was. It's one thing to be anti-religious, I remember telling Cristina after seeing this, but it's another to disguise racism against an entire ethnic group (in this case, North Africans from former French colonies like Algeria) with a progressive ideology of secularism that has its roots in the French Revolution's rebellion against the Catholic Church in 1789. "Everyone seems so confused," Cristina quietly observed.

Walking to the bed-and-breakfast that we had chosen earlier to meet some friends who'd driven down from Berlin the night before, I thought back to the reason I'd come to Paris the previous year. On the way home from my first trip to Israel in fourteen years, I had stopped in town for a week to collect literature from what was then called "*La Nouvelle Droite*" ("The New Right") for a professor I was studying Marxist intellectual history under at the time. She had been alerted to a petition circulating in French universities that year signed by a bunch of luminaries including philosopher Jacques Derrida, sociologist Pierre Bourdieu, and historian Arlette Fargue. The petition was intended to call to attention to the increasing academic legitimacy accorded to French right-wingers—in particular, neo-fascist intellectuals associated with the

National Front such as Alain de Benoist, author of the best-selling *Comment Peut-on Etre Un Peaien* (*How to Be a Pagan*) and head of the radical right-wing think tank, GRECE (*Groupement de Recherche et d'Etudes pour la Civilisation Européenne*). De Benoist had most recently caught the attention of leftist academics in the English-speaking world for his work on the political theory of Italian Communist Party founder Antonio Gramsci, and now he was introducing it to right-wing political circles in France.

My job was to pick up as many titles as I could by these writers and draft a report on how conservative scholars were attempting to engineer a "red-brown" synthesis, whereby right-wing intellectuals would draw disenfranchised post-'89 communists into the ranks of the nationalist camp. In de Benoist's case, this meant assimilating a Marxist critique of modern capitalism's erosion of European indigenous worldviews—read Paganism—by introducing monotheism to Europe through Judaism in the form of Christianity. It was argued that Europeans were being robbed of their founding cultural identity, and thus their freedom. The introduction of Islam to the continent through mass migrations from Africa, Asia, and the Middle East was merely the latest symptom of this phenomenon. Europeans had to resurrect their ancient, pre-monotheistic religions, de Benoist stated, in order to (read between the lines) restore their pure, indigenous moral community.

All the secondary literature on the subject that I photocopied at the Sorbonne library on that trip expressed indignation over the degree to which such arguments were finding common ground in the French cultural mainstream. In nearly every commentary, there was evidence of a major identity crisis on the part of the academic left. Not only was it important to out these closet fascists employing left-wing academic methodologies, but it was of equal urgency to determine once and for all "what distinguishes us from them."

Not being familiar enough with any of these concerned scholars' work at the time, I scratched my head and wondered what the real distinction was.

On the cold and rainy afternoon the day before I left, I stumbled into the Éditions Gallimard bookstore and found the latest title by Derrida sitting on the new publications table. It was the French edition of his controversial *Spectres of Marx*, in which the author announces himself to be one of the last real Marxists. Picking up the paperback and reading through the introduction, I said to myself, *Ah ha, that's it! They've decided that they're Marxists again.* I reached into my pocket, but discovered I only had enough cash for a single meal before flying home to San Francisco.

All of this came back to me on our last afternoon in Paris in 1995. Due to my dyslexic errors in calculating the exchange rate, I had just about run out of money again. After our third day of wandering, spending more time taking photographs of anti-Islamic graffiti than looking at Louis XIV-era paintings in the Louvre, Cristina and I decided to make a mad dash back to Spain. This time we took a different route, heading from Paris to the Atlantic coast, then through Pays Basque straight across the country in a twenty-four-hour marathon drive. By midnight, we had arrived at the border. It looked empty. Spanish passport and custom controls were vacant. Toll barriers were raised. We could have driven through, but I decided not to. The idea of crossing a border that didn't really exist was alien to me.

"I don't know," Cristina said in protest. "Spanish authorities might be a bit more lax about such things than the French are."

I was skeptical. The French border police had, in fact, subjected us to an identity check when we had crossed into Perpignan from Catalonia. "It just seems too weird," I replied. "Here we are, on a continent exploding with all kinds of new distinctions—ethnic, religious, cultural, political—but we can travel into another country without even passing through immigration. I don't understand it. And I don't want to get in trouble. Let's just crash here and get a fresh start in the morning."

We spent the night in the car, in a deserted parking lot adjacent to a filling station. The next morning I was woken up by the sound of a convoy of French military vehicles that had stopped for coffee, perhaps en route to another departure point for Bosnia. I scratched my eyes and looked out as the soldiers jumped from the creaky metal hulls of their camouflaged armored vehicles. Cristina was still sleeping, and I decided to place a collect call to my father in Tel Aviv.

"Abba, you won't believe what's going on here," I told him. "Ever since we left Spain there's been an amazing amount of military traffic on all the roads and highways. It seems like Europe's on the brink of war again."

"Yes, child," my father said. "I understand that NATO is getting ready to strike the Serbs, but there's been no formal declaration of hostilities yet."

"I dunno," I answered. "There's so much anti-Islamic sentiment here. I can't understand why NATO would be mobilizing to defend Bosnian Muslims."

Elie laughed quietly as he answered me. "Look, Yoel, if you only understood how concerned the Allies are about Iran becoming directly involved in Bosnia, you'd stick your neck out for these people, too. Just yesterday, some Israeli friends of mine told me that the Americans had seized several Iranian naval vessels in Croatia. They were full of Mujahedeen and military equipment destined for the Muslim army. That's why NATO is mobilizing—not because they feel obliged to defend the rights of Europe's Islamic community, but because they don't want Iran to get a foothold in Europe."

I hung up the phone, stunned by the simplicity of it all. He was right: Europe hadn't really changed that much. It was looking after its own perceived interests, as it always had. The only difference was in the explanations people were offering for why history was repeating itself. I recalled Marx's famous statement in *The Eighteenth Brumaire* that when history first repeats itself, it's a tragedy; but the second time, it's a farce. That, I realized, was the real difference. All of a sudden, the idea of crossing the border without having to show a passport to anyone seemed like the most radical thing I could do.

As we cruised freely through the abandoned border station, we saw a highway stretching out for miles before us. No tanks, no armored personnel carriers, no fighter-bombers flying overhead. Just the way it should be: empty. Sensing the irony of the situation, I sipped my first cup of coffee of the new day, gunned the accelerator, and began the final leg of our journey. For a moment it felt like I was experiencing something new.

That sense of newness is one we need to nurture. The more you learn, the easier it is to slip into mere pattern recognition. When Marx talks about history repeating itself, he is careful to show it as repetition *with a difference*. When events occur first as tragedy and then as farce, the return of the old is always complicated by the intrusion of the new. That's why I get angry when people say that a situation is reminiscent of the former Soviet Union or "just like it was under the Nazis." Yes, there are times when we need to take off our thinking caps and acknowledge the barbarism that continues to plague "civilized" societies. My cousin Francis is right to think that "genocide is genocide," but only up to a point. When invocation of the past becomes a reflex, history loses its power to instruct.

Several years ago, a friend of mine who owns an experimental record company told me that her husband would be conducting an unusual orchestra at an annual avant-garde festival in Austria called Ars Electronica, featuring DJs, effects manipulators, and Power Book players. "You have no idea how much this means to him," she said. "He's bringing his art right into the heart of what is still a fascist country." Though I didn't say anything at the time, my immediate reaction to her statement was entirely negative. There's nothing inherently radical or anti-fascist about electronica, I thought to myself as I left our meeting. It's classically avant-garde in the worst sense of the term. What was she thinking? Besides, Austria is not Germany. And the Germany of today is not the Germany of the Cold War, much less the Germany of Adolph Hitler.

As I have made clear already, I don't like it when people use words like "fascism" lightly. As the youngest child of a generation of family members decimated by the Nazis during the Holocaust, and as a student of fascist politics, such terminology makes me nervous. In punk rock circles, and even among much of America's organized left, any political body that's considered less than one-hundred-percent democratic automatically gets labeled "fascist" or "authoritarian."

It sometimes seems that progressives refuse to be specific because they want to indict their opponents with a term that has historical resonance and symbolic moral weight, and one that everyone can easily understand. Nonetheless, having been a participant in progressive political circles for most of my adult life, I'm not sure that this is the primary reason why so many people employ the F-word so readily. Rather, as I grow older I become more convinced that it's a symptom of sloppy political thinking. The danger is that people will fail to appreciate the moral and ideological distinctions between different kinds of politics. Somehow, if we are able to understand what threatens us more precisely, we might be in a position to better advance certain progressive causes.

Of course, there's also the danger that my reaction to the F-word will become a reflex, too. I don't want to ignore the lesson I learned in France. Nor do I think people must be experts in the use of political terminology if they want to make a point. There must be some middle ground between the absurd idea that everything one dislikes is "fascist" and the tendency of over-educated theoreticians like myself to miss the forest for the trees. A number of recent events have convinced me to be a little less judgmental about such things, among them the 1999 election of Jorg Haider's extremely conservative Freedom Party to Austria's governing coalition. While Haider did not become Austria's chancellor, his figure loomed large. He has been mentioned so frequently in the news over the past few years that, while he never became more than a provincial governor, one could easily get the impression that he exercises moral leadership over the whole country. Inevitably, Haider has been discussed as though he represents the return of Europe's fascist past. After all, he has made many statements sympathetic to the Nazis: Austrian veterans of the Waffen SS are "decent people," Hitler's economic policies were "orderly," etc. Haider has also used Nazi-era terms such as "over-foreignization" to describe his objections to Austria's immigration policies. Just turn him on and let him show his Swastika-tarred feathers: Haider fits the stereotype.

At the time of Haider's ascent, the conservative political party that dominated Germany's post-war political order, the Christian Democratic Union, was in the throes of the worst political scandal to engulf the country since the Second World War. Former chancellor Helmut Kohl admitted to having ignored Germany's coveted democratic constitution by refusing to disclose the source of over one million dollars in covert payments to his party. He would not budge, because he saw the honor of keeping his word to the donors as being more important than respecting the constitution.

While this did not represent a return to fascist politics in the same way as the rise of Haider's party in Austria, the Nazi suspension of the Weimar Republic's democratic constitution in 1933 hovered in the background. Given Germany's recent history, it was a remarkable transgression. But compared to the overly dramatic Haider, Kohl received relatively lenient treatment. To be sure, he was lambasted in the press as the scandal ran its course. Yet the possibility that he might have taken the first step down the same path as Hitler was barely discussed.

Kohl, along with several other prominent CDU leaders, had trampled on the sacred core of Germany's post-fascist, democratic political identity. This created a major power vacuum on the right. A discredited Christian Democratic party, it was feared, would be replaced by a more extreme right-wing organization in the mold of Haider's organization, like the National Democratic Party. Or the CDU would feel the pressure to move itself to the right, especially given the co-optation of its historically free-market orientation by the governing Social Democrats. CDU General Secretary Laurenz Meyer's call for a renewal of German cultural values and a reassertion of national pride prior to the March 2001 state elections suggests such a possibility.

Although Germany was being governed by an ostensibly leftist coalition led by Social Democrat Gerhard Shroeder, it could hardly have been described as a socialist state. Like many of the "Third Way" liberals of the 1990s, Shroeder is already so conservative—putting the needs of big business first, chipping away at the welfare state by privatizing Germany's generous public pension program—that in light of the CDU scandal, the transformation of German politics threatened a serious moral crisis. With the old German left growing more conservative, it seemed likely that the CDU would indeed be pushed, at least rhetorically speaking, into the national camp occupied by the extreme right. In some respects, Austria's problems were minimal in comparison. Fears of an anti-democratic renewal in the heart of formerly fascist Europe, such as those harbored by my American music label friend, ultimately had some validity.

This all came to a head for me one morning as I lay in bed reading a story in the *New York Times Sunday Magazine* about Konrad Latte, a German Jewish conductor who had survived the Second World War due to the kindness of anti-fascist classical musicians in Berlin. The purpose of the article was to deflate some of the broad implications of Daniel Goldhagen's bestseller, *Hitler's Willing Executioners*. Goldhagen essentially argued that the Holocaust occurred because anti-Semitism was a prejudice endemic to nearly every sphere of German society, not just the SS and Hitler's other fanatical cadres, as many of us have been led to believe. Pointing out the numerous musicians and conductors who helped prevent Latte from falling into Nazi hands, the author of the *Times* piece wanted to show that there were many Germans who did not fit into Goldhagen's less-than-forgiving political framework.

As I read about a particularly gifted patron of Latte's who had sacrificed a promising career conducting because he refused to play in front of the Nazi leadership, I was reminded of what my label-owner friend had said the previous summer, and how I'd reacted to her. I could see her husband wanting to become a latter-day incarnation of that same conductor. Instead of directing an orchestra of woodwinds, strings, and brass playing Strauss waltzes, he was supervising an ensemble of African- and Asian-American DJs, Japanese noise merchants, European computer nerds, and Jewish dub musicians creating collage-like sound representations of a more democratic, multicultural world.

For a long and painful moment, I felt quite stupid. Nothing is ever as simple as it first seems, I reminded myself, least of all culture's relationship to politics. When art is at its critical best, it generates images of better worlds that may not be historically real, but at least possible in the realm of ideas. That's a hell of a lot better than not having such thoughts at all, especially in a musical counterculture whose professed radical politics tend to be superficial and cliché-ridden. I suddenly felt hopeful; indeed, inspired. These folks may not have had a command of all the right buzzwords, I thought. But somehow they knew what they were doing, and they were much more politically sensitive than most hardcore American leftists would be. Even if the project they were involved in was still just a feeling, a metaphor trying to overcome its own impulsive and heartfelt abstraction, it was far superior to blissful ignorance. This process of reeducating myself brought me to a final question. In the end, what's worse: to see injustice and brutality and call it "fascism" or to not see it all?

P.O. Box 7154 Olympia WA 98507 USA
ph (360) 352-8565 fax (360) 786-5024
retail@kpunk.com

To: Joel Schalit 08/24/98

From: Jon Quittner

Dear Joel – there is pain in my heart… For I have to return the greater portion of these Christal Methodists CDs unsold. You know the Methodistas are the gerbil of my eye; I tried like hell to express that to the kids (and the grumpy-ass buyers & whatnot who are their masters) but it mattered not… The few we did sell were mailorders through our website, and that sort of illustrates the problem as far as stores – they never could figure out whether to put these in the punk section, the electronica section, the spoken word section or what… If they had a freaky post-punk kill-christians iconoclast section that'd be one thing. But no. It was not to be. Who was it that said "so and so and their times" was a lame title for a biography, because anyone worth biographasizing would have a biography entitled "so and so versus their times"? Alas then.

Take care,

DOWN AND OUT WITH ROCK AND ROLL

The limitations of contemporary progressive thought in America are sometimes so pervasive that even those on the cultural "fringe" fall victim. In this regard, what disturbed me most about Nirvana's breakthrough in the early 1990s was the apparent impact that the group's success had on other people's lives. I had nothing against the band; I bought their first album when it came out. I taped early singles like "Love Buzz" and "Sliver" when they arrived as promos at the college radio station where I worked in Portland. Not to mention that, while at the Pine Street Theater during a Screaming Trees concert in early 1990, Kurt Cobain (Nirvana's singer/guitarist) saved me from the hands of an angry skinhead who was beating me up because he didn't like my new dye job.

"Are you okay?" asked Kurt, after he delivered a swift karate kick to my fashion-conscious assailant's bald head.

"Yeah," I said, a little dazed, "thanks."

"No problem, man. If the Nazi bugs you again, gimme a holler." Kurt blended back into the crowd to watch the Screaming Trees as they roared into the epic "Black Sun Rising," eventually getting carried away by the swelling crowd that had not yet made him a rock star.

Two years after that show, I had, like many people in alternative music communities, become obsessed with the media circus surrounding Nirvana. Something about it made me very uncomfortable. It had become almost impossible to get a glimpse of the "real" Nirvana. The band had been pushed into the vanguard position of a consumer revolution. Most of the people clamoring for a taste of Seattle had only the slightest clue what bands like Nirvana meant to the fans in the community from which they had emerged. And I wanted people to know this. The band's wagon was about to collapse under the weight of the false believers.

One day, after reading Re/Search's *Pranks* in the Berkeley library bathroom between theology classes, I decided to engage in a little experiment. I got on the telephone to my old college friend, Surfer Bill, because his disinterested, out-of-breath voice reminded me of Cobain's. I told Surfer Bill I had this idea that we should call up local modern-rock stations and record stores pretending to be Kurt. He would inquire about promotional opportunities in the Bay Area in advance of Nirvana headlining a benefit concert for Bosnian rape victims. The benefit line-up also included the Breeders, L7, and the Disposable Heroes of Hiphoprisy.

Amused, Surfer Bill agreed. After drinking a few microbrews he'd brought down from a recent trip to Portland, we got on the telephone and started calling numbers from the phone book. I posed as a Sub Pop Records rep doing a study of sales patterns among punk retailers in the Bay Area. (Sub Pop is the independent label to which Nirvana was signed before they moved on to Geffen Records, a major label.) I called The Gap looking for the authentic Calvin Klein grungewear I'd read about in the *San Francisco Chronicle*. Surfer Bill rang every radio station we could think of until one of them bought our shtick and allowed him to record several station identifications, which he perfunctorily fucked up, making sure he sounded as bored by the whole process as possible.

"Listen, I don't have all day," Surfer Bill said to one friendly program director. "Contrary to what some stupid people here think, Sub Pop doesn't have all that much money. Despite the hype, they're still a poor punk label and it makes me really mad to hear people saying Sub Pop's become such a yuppie outfit. I feel bad about running up their Sprint bill calling radio stations in California all day."

"That's totally cool, Kurt," said the program director. "We gotta keep those indie labels from going in the red. We'll speed this up so you can go home. Would you like me to call you back?"

"Naw," said Surfer Bill, "I gotta few lines here Jonathan and Bruce gave me to recite so I'm just gonna deliver 'em and go home if you don't mind."

It worked. A week after calling the stations I thought were the worst offenders of my sensibilities, I heard Surfer Bill's voice on the radio in between Salt-N-Pepa and Wham, saying, "This is Kurt Cobain, and whenever I'm in San Francisco, I support the SF Needle exchange." It was my way of fighting back. Before addressing what it was that I was fighting against, it is important to first examine the economic history that led to the market triumph of "punk" and otherwise alternative rock music.

It's difficult to explain the resuscitation of the American recording industry in the early 1990s. The glory days of the 1960s were largely a product of the rising economic tide during the Cold War, fueled by a military boom. By the time acts like Nirvana hit the charts, America had already experienced two recessions in recent history:

the first in the mid-1970s, as a result of the Arab Oil Embargo and the crippling inflation caused by the Nixon Administration's mishandling of the economy; and the second, in the early 1980s, due to the Reagan administration's radical deregulation of the market and its lowering of interest rates. As the eighties drew to a close, Americans had new reasons to be anxious. After the relative peace and prosperity in the middle of the decade, the Iran-Contra scandal ended the Reagan years on a sour note. By the time George Bush (senior) had settled into the White House, the stability of the Cold War was disintegrating. The collapse of the Eastern Bloc, the uprising in Tiananmen Square, and the Gulf War all signaled the dawn of a "New World Order" shadowed by uncertainty. On top of that, the economy was once again dropping off. And despite all of the world's trouble spots, the American military was faced with massive cutbacks in spending. This time around, the success of "hard" popular music couldn't be attributed to the affluence of a self-satisfied warfare state. The only common denominator with the 1960s was large sales figures.

In 1991, *Billboard* magazine changed the surveying system used to compile its charts. Suddenly, previously marginal rap and punk rock acts were able to score number-one records with relative ease. The recording industry was turned upside down. Money that used to be reserved for safe pop artists was redirected toward bands that would have previously been a record executive's worst nightmare.

Although the effects of this change were felt most dramatically in the world of rap, the revival of the mainstream recording industry had the greatest impact on rock. Many of the biggest selling rap artists remained on independent labels, as most majors were unwilling to defend the extreme content of their songs against outraged politicians and consumers. Hard rock was safer by comparison, not least because it was rooted in a genre with a track record from the industry's heyday in the sixties. The irony of this situation is that modern bands like Nirvana benefited equally from their proximity to, and their distance from, their forbears like Led Zeppelin. On some level, even conservative Baby Boomers were used to loud, "shocking" music with a trippy edge.

The rise of the "classic rock" radio programming format during the 1980s played a major role here. Unknowingly conspiring with one another to create a renaissance of production and consumption, punk and classic rock came together for the first time with the ascendance of "grunge." Even as some Baby Boomers refused to listen to records made after the 1970s, the more adventurous members of their generation—most importantly, music critics and industry insiders—enthusiastically embraced Nirvana, Pearl Jam, the Stone Temple Pilots, and Soundgarden. Grunge took the hard rock of the sixties and seventies that had been burned deeper into the collective unconscious of the American public by classic-rock radio programming and combined it with the aesthetics and grass roots, community-based business strategies pioneered and developed by punk-rock record companies. As a result, the recording industry was able to expand its massive infrastructure into the intimate, local sphere of economic activity opened up by small, independent labels.

"What is the real significance of Nirvana?" This was the consummate question for rock music in the early 1990s. People who were unable to agree on much of anything shared a desire to answer it. I was certainly one of them. As I've already suggested, I never deluded myself into believing that the band's 1991 breakthrough constituted a revolution in the music business. Nonetheless, my own connection to the culture of the Pacific Northwest made

Nirvana more important to me than my mild enthusiasm for their music would imply. Simply put, Nirvana impacted me because they meant so much to people in my world. Even if I wasn't seduced by the hype, I wanted to know why so many others were. And, conversely, I also wanted to know why the self-proclaimed "true" punks reading *Maximum Rock and Roll* (a monthly fanzine based in San Francisco) were so fixated on Nirvana, despite the fact that they were so ready to label the band "sell outs."

I had been a loyal reader of *MRR* since the early eighties. But by the time Nirvana hit it big, I had soured on the magazine's ideological line. Its definition of punk seemed to get narrower with each passing minute. So much of the music and art that had made punk interesting to me in the first place—the studio experimentation of bands like Crass and the early Butthole Surfers, the collage aesthetic reflected in album covers by Winston Smith and Gee Vaucher, the desire to make listeners confront their own prejudices head on—had been exiled from *MRR*'s pages. Working at college radio stations when Public Enemy and other rap acts burst on the scene, and listening to all of the excellent independent music that defied classification in record store bins, I realized that there was more to life than the short, loud, angry guitar rock being promoted in *MRR* as though it were the new socialist realism. I also came to see that there were other more thought-provoking means of critiquing the mainstreaming of the music coming from Seattle than by reiterating the cry of "sell out" over a relentlessly simpleminded editorial beat.

Groundbreaking records by European artists not traditionally regarded as being part of *MRR's* official "punk" canon questioned the political orthodoxies of the counterculture and represented a deepening awareness that musical radicalism is more often than not merely another alienated response to life in market-driven societies. One such album was Laibach's 1988 EP, *Sympathy for the Devil*, in which these former Yugoslavian agit-proppers offered up eight entirely different covers of the Rolling Stones' classic take on the spirit of capitalism manifesting itself throughout the ages as the devil—replete with samples taken from Jean-Luc Godard's similarly titled quasi-documentary about the Stones. Not only was *Sympathy* self-conscious of the integral relationship between economics and culture, it was also hysterically funny and self-mocking in a way that American leftists could rarely be.

I bathed in the sounds of these records; an album like *Sympathy* gave me a sense that there was indeed another side to protest music far beyond the humorless moralisms and unimaginative lock-step artistic limits of the community in which I had first learned about anti-capitalism. Indeed, as compelling a piece of music as the original Rolling Stones song remains, by the late 1980s it had become encumbered by the band's status as a permanent fixture in the highly commercialized mainstream rock music market. The group's past achievements were constantly regurgitated for a rapidly aging listening audience by classic rock radio stations in the United States. By taking on this song and recasting it in eight different ways, sometimes even more mind-numbing than the original, Laibach (a band named after the Nazi-era designation of its hometown, Ljubliana, during the Second World War) had assumed the voice of the so-called enemy and turned this piece of work back into a vehicle of protest.

That's in part how I came up with the idea for the prank my friend Bill and I pulled on Bay Area radio stations. What I saw in Nirvana's success was an opportunity to point out the insincerity of the punk idea that musicians were common people who wanted to be just like their fans. By impersonating Kurt Cobain, we thought, we would be reversing the effects of having our identity commodified by the false bohemian advertising surrounding Nirvana's success. If Nirvana really were an everyman's band that represented the yearnings of a generation—expressing all of their rage, sorrow, hopelessness, and shame just as Seattle magazines like *The Rocket* told me they were—then I had the right to take on Kurt's identity and feed this nonsense back to Geffen Records executives, *Time*, Sub Pop, *Rolling Stone*, and even Kurt himself. Somewhere, somehow, I thought he'd approve of it. I said to myself, if these people are telling me that punk is now acceptable, that my generation is finally being heard, that Kurt of all people is our spokesperson, then I'm gonna do exactly what they tell me to. I'm gonna exercise my right to be a punk and fool them at their own game.

In 1996, two years after Kurt Cobain's suicide and five years after Nirvana's album *Nevermind* first entered *Billboard*'s top ten, the smoke screen surrounding the band's significance began to clear. We were no longer subject to the endless barrage of daily pronouncements by rock magazines, music journalists, and weekly newspapers that we were in the midst of a cultural revolution spearheaded by three young working-class men from Seattle. Perhaps the war over selling out was over. But who had won?

The only way to answer that question, again, is to figure out what we were fighting about. Unfortunately, most participants on "my" side never bothered with that difficult task. They were content to do battle on the basis of a diffuse desire to become part of the mainstream. To be sure, there are compelling arguments for breaking free of a position on the musical margins of society. But the reasoning will inevitably prove hollow unless people consider the terms under which this move toward the middle takes place. This is what the more thoughtful critics of selling out were trying to say. For the most part, however, the critics denounced by rote all attempts at becoming popular, without taking the time to differentiate between individual cases—Hüsker Dü, Sonic Youth, Nirvana, Pearl Jam, Green Day, the Offspring, and many others. This accusation can even be leveled at recording artist and producer Steve

Albini, whose famous piece, "The Problem With Music," in the independent journal *The Baffler* charts the rise and fall of a hypothetical rock band that decides to go major.

Was this merely the struggle of twenty-somethings eager to be recognized as legitimate consumers by the establishment? Or were we fooling ourselves into believing that we were really engaged in class conflict? It wasn't hard for some writers to identify a Marxist model of successful working-class revolution in the story of Nirvana's breakthrough and the bands that followed in its wake. This spin, naturally, made me quite irritable: If this was the only way to fulfill dreams of a better life, there was little hope left for meaningful politics. You have to imagine political change in order to work for it. With the explosion of "alternative culture" in the early 1990s, it seemed that people could only imagine change in terms of their consumer status.

Obviously, the idea that you could buy your way to freedom was not an invention of the early 1990s. The contradictions of alternative consumption simply became more acute in Nirvana's wake. But they were already an integral part of punk rock. In retrospect, it seems strange that it took so long for punk to be incorporated into mainstream American culture. The economic downturn that began in the early 1970s had a significant impact on the initial marginalization of punk from mainstream music production, promotions, and sales. Despite reasonably successful experiments with groups like the Dead Boys, the Sex Pistols, Richard Hell, the Gang of Four, and the Buzzcocks, major labels were not interested in producing and marketing punk bands in the early eighties; evidently, most labels lacked the promotional imagination necessary to succeed commercially with these borderline groups in a large and segmented music market.

Sales weren't the only problem. An early major-label schism with American punk groups the Dead Kennedys and Black Flag centered around the cancellation of their contracts with IRS and Unicorn/MCA over what ultimately amounted to censorship of artistic content. Neither firm wanted to market or distribute bands that appeared to promote radical politics. In Black Flag's case, this anxiety was entirely misplaced; for the most part, the band was merely mobilizing bourgeois resentment against low forms of consumer culture, which it attacked with a mean-spirited, albeit amusing vengeance. The Dead Kennedys, on the other hand, really did have a political program, based on an anti-fascist critique of American everyday life that was as artistically compelling as it was historically on target. As a consequence of their rejection by the majors in the early eighties, both groups started their own groundbreaking record companies, SST and Alternative Tentacles. It was these labels, more than the musicians who founded them—particularly in the case of SST—that laid the foundation for the independent music scene of the last twenty years. Together, SST and AT defined their basic principles: a willingness to critique the banality of mainstream mass culture, a theory of entrepreneurial economic decentralization, and a do-it-yourself aesthetic with wide appeal for middle-class adolescents and college students seeking to reshape their "over-produced" lives.

All the ingredients for the laments about selling out in the early nineties were already present in the heyday of these pioneering firms. But regardless of the reality concealed behind their impressive façades—SST was notorious for not paying royalties to its bands and Alternative Tentacles, as I will discuss later, had problems of its own—these labels benefited enormously from the cosmetic powers of hindsight. From the perspective of someone battered with the music of third-rate Nirvana clones in today's musical landscape, the early 1980s look like a Golden Age. It didn't matter whether SST and AT actually carried out the ideals they promoted. It didn't even matter whether they were the right ideals to be promoting.

Part of the problem, of course, is that these principles were divorced from any connection to a world outside of music. They became exclusively aesthetic. Instead of bemoaning the political realities of American life, self-righteous indie rockers of the early nineties were largely content to complain about how the quality of music is necessarily compromised by multinational relations of production. The most dangerous aspect of this narrowing of focus is that it makes it extremely difficult to understand punk's compatibility with capitalism: its modes of production, its cultural institutions, and its administrative functions in modern society. After all, none of the early indie labels of the 1980s were in the business of giving music away for free. To clarify what was at stake, it is necessary to go back to the concepts of labor and mode-of-production which lie at the heart of American punk ideology.

Having been shut out of the productive process of mainstream American popular music, punk intellectuals such as Dead Kennedys singer Jello Biafra and *Maximum Rock and Roll* editor Tim Yohannon (now deceased) formulated an economic strategy by which they were able to construct their own artistic institutions and markets. They didn't have to worry so much about how to disseminate their music and literature to the masses, because they were creating a captive audience. The strategies that they adopted paralleled those of the new social movements in the 1960s and 1970s, which attempted to politicize cultural institutions as though they were pre-revolutionary autonomous zones. The goal was to turn those establishments into resources which could help people resist the political authority of an increasingly interventionist state bureaucracy that was limiting the capacity of individuals to think freely for themselves and in association with others.

The decision by American punks to adopt strategies from an earlier time was a response to the economic marginalization imposed upon artists within a fairly conservative and aesthetically unsophisticated popular artistic tradition. Where there was sufficient critical mass, this dynamic led to the construction of a self-sustaining punk community. Tim Yohannon, a member of the Communist Party and a former student activist at Rutgers during the sixties, created *Maximum Rock and Roll* with precisely this goal in mind. He set out to politicize an industry with the potential, from his perspective, to serve an important function for young and old people alike. Yohannon hoped punk rock would become a place to reconstruct the political idealism he had absorbed during the student movement.

The cornerstone of the new punk ideology, as defined in *MRR*, was a call to reject all overtures from the mainstream. Ideally, punks should write music for themselves and their friends; produce it independently, utilizing all the means at their disposal; and manage their own business affairs in order to retain control over the creative and political aspects of their work. As this ideology took hold, small record companies such as SST and Alternative Tentacles eventually grew larger, signed new artists, and bred a class of indie-music bureaucrats who fulfilled the administrative roles that artists within the community had been urged to assume themselves. Subsequently, the notions of aesthetic, productive, and administrative autonomy went out the window, and what emerged was a petite-bourgeois imitation of the economic and social organization of the mainstream music business, whose purpose was to manufacture and disseminate popular music on a wider scale.

The co-optation of the new punk counter-hegemony was inevitable. In their struggle to establish sustainable institutions, punk record companies and magazines targeted new segments of the music market previously ignored by the entertainment conglomerates. Having identified exploitable shopping outlets such as privately owned record stores, clubs, mail order catalogues, and L.L. Bean–style 1-800 credit card order services, punk institutions began to compete with the very firms they were seeking independence from. Accordingly, larger labels began looking at the possibility of moving into such markets as a response to the competition posed by punk rock.

By 1986, the minor financial success of independent labels like Enigma, Rough Trade, and SST had convinced major label executives that an economic infrastructure now existed which could support their expansion into a controversial fringe market for new music. The results of this initial dalliance with the indie world were not promising. Even though major labels started by signing groups with extensive sales histories such as the Replacements, Hüsker Dü, and Soul Asylum—all, notably, from the same Minneapolis music scene—they had a hard time turning a consistent profit. But one of the strongest impacts of these signings was indirect—the effect on music journalism. No matter how commercially marginal a band like Hüsker Dü may have seemed in a major-label context, the legitimacy of being on a big label in and of itself made it more acceptable for critics in mainstream magazines and newspapers to write about the music of the rock underground.

This helps to explain how a new generation of rock criticism consolidated itself in the 1980s, as relative old-timers like Greil Marcus and Robert Christgau welcomed younger writers like Greg Tate, Neil Strauss, Gina Arnold, and Ann Powers. In another era, these talented writers would probably have been contributing literary reviews to the *New Yorker*, *The New Republic*, or *The Nation*. But now the cutting edge for criticism had been displaced into the music world. Even when writers like these were not championing indie (or formerly indie) rock bands, they were making room for the mainstreaming of alternative culture in a broader sense.

Something was in the air. And despite the cautionary tales offered by the Replacements and Hüsker Dü, staunchly independent punk groups like Sonic Youth began to entertain the idea of signing major-label contracts. They had good reasons for making the leap. Why remain poor and impoverished on an independent label when they could be receiving better pay elsewhere? A band with its shit together might be able to devote more time to perfecting its music with a major-label advance, even if it meant going into debt to its label. The economy was also a factor. In the midst of corporate America's romance with downsizing, the chance that an artist might land a tolerable "real" job to support her art seemed increasingly remote. Musicians had to preserve their livelihood. Acutely aware of the exaggerated effects that the weak economy of the late eighties was having on small businesses, bands began leaving independent labels in droves.

The furor over "going major" reached its peak in the years following Nirvana's unexpected success. I found the discussion of selling out as depressing as the actions of the bands who were accused of it. And that's a major reason why I spent the better part of the nineties hating rock and roll. It didn't matter what kind of rock it was. Hardcore, surf, garage, punk: it all seemed corrupt and shallow. I stopped buying records. I stopped listening to the radio. I became frightened at the prospect of opening weekly newspapers and discovering the "next big thing." I even quit going to shows. Nothing annoyed me more than having to sit in smoky bars full of well-dressed, cliquish, drunken people, waiting several hours for the arrogant headliner to appear. Or going to the record

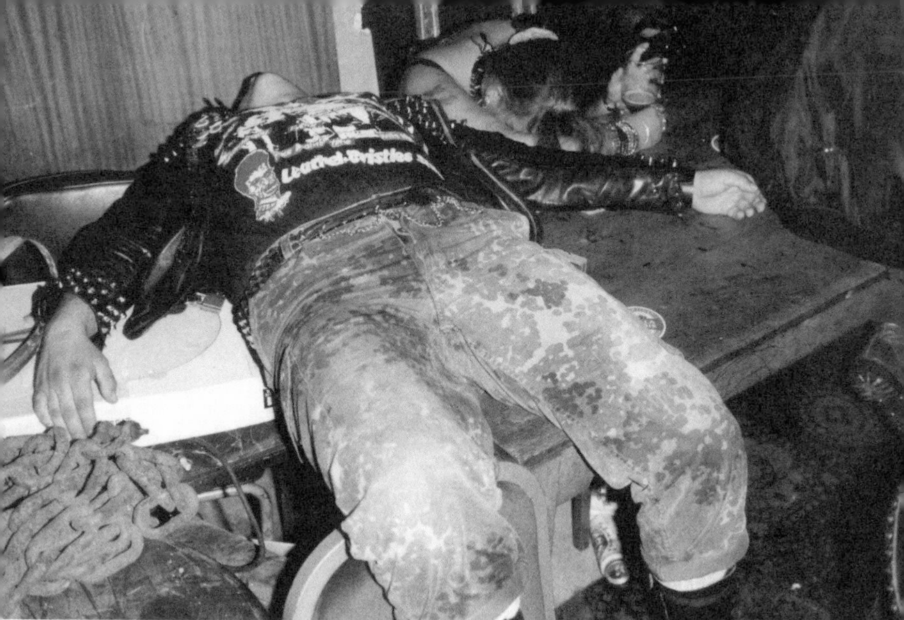

Drunk punks, London, England, 1999

store and having to wade through thousands of CDs and 7"s only to walk out with a record I'd loathe once I had the chance to listen to it properly.

But when I try to understand why I reacted to rock and roll so negatively in this period, I find once again that I need to look to the past. I'm convinced that it was the economic and cultural changes taking place that had earlier led me to get more involved in the music business. Straight out of college in 1990, I got a radio-promotion job at an indie label where it was never quite clear whether I was an intern or a wage slave. I rarely got paid. Artists we promoted, like the Swans' Michael Gira, yelled at me when I pronounced their last names incorrectly. And the bands we worked with were never quite to my taste. It was totally depressing.

The problem was that I desperately wanted to be involved. During the mid 1980s, there seemed to be something so revolutionary about punk rock. I was sure that by getting into the business I would be helping to create a better culture. I was such a good punk leftist, dressed in ill-fitting but fashionable thrift-store clothing and spouting erudite lines about the evil culture industry. But I didn't quite understand that being a fan is one thing and getting involved in the economic side of the business is entirely different. I think the mistake I made at the time was assuming that I could hold my nose and not be bothered by the filth and grime that is an integral part of any business, even punk rock.

Sadly, it took me a long while to figure this out. By the time I got savvy, I'd wasted so many precious hours that I could have spent teaching myself real skills for a real job, where the chances of being exploited by employers were actually far lower. After quitting my job as a radio publicist, I went back to graduate school and started working part-time at college radio stations again, only to find myself right in the middle of one of the most important media outlets for the alternative cultural boom of the early 1990s. Back inside the belly of the beast, there was no escape.

Free dinners and long, personal conversations with lonely publicists have never tangibly helped cash-poor radio workers surviving by the skin of their teeth. Every time one of these publicists called, I'd sit there and reassure myself over and over again that I hadn't been as insincere and patronizing as these people were when I had been in their unfortunate shoes. Twenty-five free Seaweed CD-single covers of a Fleetwood Mac song? No thanks. I hated Fleetwood Mac in the seventies, and I saw no irony in covering them in the nineties. But freebies are freebies, and cunning record companies always have plenty of crap to share.

If I couldn't figure out what to do with these soon-to-be cocktail coasters, my music-director boss sure as hell could, because he was volunteering thirty hours each week at a dead-end job. So it was imperative that he work publicists to some personal advantage. If he was charming enough, the label might even hire him. But the chances weren't good. For every music director who got hired as an A&R rep (a position vaguely resembling a "talent scout") by a record label, ten of them didn't, and there was no way to know whether you were going to be the lucky one. Unless you were independently wealthy and simply donating your well-meaning time, you had to play the game and hope like hell you weren't going to end up an even bigger sucker in the end.

The potential for scoring some personal advantage was too present. It contaminated everything we did. The whole situation turned into such a transparent spectacle that it was hard to take seriously after a while. That is, unless you didn't have a personal stake in it. It was intense watching people take advantage of each other all across the underground cultural spectrum. College radio served as ground zero for this insidious chain of self-promoting corruption. After meetings to discuss which groups we were going to promote at the station during such and such a week, I'd sit there sipping my coffee and wondering why all my co-workers were giving all these undeserving, abstract label logos in far away cities their free labor. What disturbed me even more was how naturally it all happened. Twenty years earlier, they would have been gearing up to take on The Man. But there was no consideration of the greater political picture in the alternative-culture industry of the nineties, least of all with regard to labor exploitation (as I will discuss later in this chapter). The fall of the Berlin Wall, the Gulf War, Somalia, ethnic cleansing, homelessness, joblessness, NAFTA, the Christian Coalition, Waco: Who gave a shit? There seemed to be a tacit understanding that politics was no longer a concern in rock and roll. Our task was to redistribute artistic capital, plain and simple. The train had already left the station, and our only imperative was to keep up with it before we were left too far behind.

The real issue wasn't selling out to majors. It was selling music in the first place. Long before Nirvana was a sparkle in David Geffen's eye, the defenders of independent music at America's college radio stations had already sold everything they had to sell, except their labor, which they gave away for free. Although the early nineties made matters worse by turning college radio into a minor league for the major labels, the damage had already been done.

Grunge music couldn't outlive the market it rejuvenated in the early nineties because it was never enough of a coherent musical genre to transcend its punk and hard rock predecessors. Kurt Cobain's suicide in the spring of 1994 symbolically terminated the period of unprecedented economic growth in the alternative music industry that was inaugurated by the success of Jane's Addiction's 1989 LP, *Nothing's Shocking*. Despite the success stories of Nirvana's bastard offspring—such as Bad Company–soundalikes Everclear and sugarcoated Nirvana clone Bush—grunge had faded into its own convenient break-even high school niche market by 1996.

The music industry fell back into its traditional red-tape crisis mode when its investments ceased to bring in overwhelmingly profitable returns. Now it was back to spending more money on music videos than records, dropping bands who failed to move less than a hundred thousand units, and buying significant interests in alternative labels like Sub Pop and Matador for their back catalogues (instead of for their projected future returns). Two of the only reminders of the alternative bull market that could still be heard were Green Day's nouveau-riche Billy Joe crying out about how boring it was to be stuck in a filthy apartment off of Telegraph Avenue in Berkeley; and the repetitive sharpening of swords at *Maximum Rock and Roll* HQ in San Francisco, where editor Tim Yohannon derided the morality of the labels he had helped foster, like Epitaph, for their commercial successes. This was the punk-rock equivalent of factional infighting amongst upper-middle-class Trotskyites over revolutionary strategies. Predictably, ignorance abounded in the underground. No one could differentiate between revolutionary marketing strategies and political rhetoric, so the real terms of the selling-out debate became a grand, rudderless melodrama.

Nevertheless, Yohannon and his burrito-hungry band of teen cultists could safely argue in the mid-nineties that their advice against straying into shopping malls was still relevant. Politics had finally transcended marketing, and someone had actually killed himself over his inability to reconcile commercial success with cultural authenticity. Driving the point home with the subtlety of a cruise missile, Yohannon began his thoughtful indictment of his rebellious progeny by printing a picture of a faceless person with a cocked revolver stuck in their mouth in the first issue of *MRR* after Cobain took his own life.

Soon, punks began pointing their fingers at each other in a confused and misguided attempt to identify scapegoats for their market clout. Goaded by *MRR*'s increasingly hostile denunciations of Jello Biafra and his independent record label for creating the recipe that made punk profitable, homeless crusties descended upon Biafra at the famous Gilman Street club in Berkeley, beating him savagely for being a rock star and a sell out. Nothing better epitomized the conservative and reactionary tendencies of punk politics.

Redistributing cultural goods is not the same as redistributing wealth, and it never will be. Unfortunately, Biafra had never really taken the time to explain this to his audience. (The name of his record label, Alternative Tentacles, should have been a clue.) But the powerful political message of Biafra's lyrics deluded too many people into thinking that the label was itself a political project. Biafra was held accountable for destroying a countercultural movement that had never really understood him, let alone itself. A terrible irony of Biafra's plight is that his own denunciation of right-wing punks in the Dead Kennedys' seminal "Nazi Punks Fuck Off" had been turned against him. Maybe punk rockers were the wrong people to be proselytizing to after all.

Not long after this brutal incident, punk entered its apparent final stage of influence on the mainstream music market. Southern California's "pop punk" band, the Offspring, topped the American music charts in 1994 with an album released by Epitaph Records. Predictably, their stunning success—unprecedented for an independent rock band—prodded them to seek out a major-label deal. But Epitaph was as much to blame as the band for the split. After selling eight million copies of the group's fourth LP, *Smash*, Epitaph allegedly began to treat the group as though they were a commodity. One publication reported that label-head and ex–Bad Religion guitarist Brett Gurewitz had gone so far as to take out a life insurance policy on lead singer Dexter Holland. Another story contended that Gurewitz had sold all of Epitaph's publishing rights to Sony Music without informing any of the artists on the label.

In an interview, singer Holland explained that the Offspring had found out about changes at the label through stories in the *Los Angeles Times*. Holland argued that the band was moving to a major because Gurewitz had effectively sold them to one anyway. The singer contended that by terminating their contract and moving to Columbia Records on their own accord, the group was in fact taking back control over the fruits of their labor. They would have preferred to remain on their independent label,

Holland added, had they been treated more like friends and less like products.

Whatever the legitimacy of Holland's assertions—and I suspect he was telling the truth—the most poignant aspect of this story is the way it blurs the distinction between independent and major labels. Greed infects the music industry, just like it does any other business. One problem with punk ideologies of independence and economic autonomy is that they are founded on the conviction that it is possible to engage in certain kinds of business practices without becoming too focused on marketing strategies. And it's not just labels that try to raise the value of their artists; many bands also search for every possible way to do this. Ideally, this quest would only be expressed through better songwriting. But few musicians are ever fully rewarded for the amount of time they put into their songs. And the market for music is never lucrative enough to guarantee that recording artists can live exclusively off of their work. So musicians constantly find themselves—like their labels—trying to find new ways to profit by their music. Even the most politically radical artists, unless they have another source of income, are faced with a series of contradictions between their ideals and how they earn a living. Nevertheless, fans and critics alike continue to be shocked when bands do things like accept product endorsements or license songs to be used in car commercials.

While the magazine editor in me is delighted to pick up stories that hammer home the point that artists are not immune to certain kinds of failings, the leftist in me has grown tired of continuously being reminded that people still buy into the idea that punk is somehow inherently anti-capitalist. What I always want to tell my colleagues is that we have to stop elevating art above the economy, since it leads to a perverse idolatry whereby commodities and the companies that produce them become objects of inappropriately displaced frustration. There is a fundamental lack of understanding about the limits of cultural activism in a market-driven economy. Besides, punk's real target was never capitalism *per se*, but a mass-produced culture that discourages people from acting in their own self-interest. It has always been all or nothing. And that's what made punk ideology such a disappointment in the 1990s. When there are no finer distinctions than "us" versus "them," it becomes almost impossible to inspire meaningful action in a real world where each one of us is both "us" *and* "them."

Over the past decade, our perception of the utopian possibilities punk once promised has had to accommodate this painful realization. We ceased believing that the bands signed to major labels in Nirvana's wake would deliver on their revolutionary promise of a better tomorrow. We've finally understood that they never knew what they were going to free us from in the first place. The paradox is that punk lives on: Not only do major-label acts like Green Day continue to sell a large number of albums, but the perversely obscure bands that have always graced the pages of *Maximum Rock and Roll* are still alive and kicking, too. The persistence of style makes up for lack of original, "essential" punk content. The shows will still get booked, the fanzines will still be written, and there will always be something to complain about.

Many people continue to begrudgingly admire groups like Green Day, Rancid, and the Offspring because their mainstream presence reminds us of a time when there were more clearly demarcated lines in politics—when it was possible to distinguish between right and left. But, in a sense, this points to where all the trouble started: After the 1960s, many people began to confuse rock bands with political vehicles. While early punk bands like Crass, the Mekons, the Clash, and the Dead Kennedys sang about capitalism with the sensitivity of Marxist philosophers, they avoided ties to disciplined revolutionary organizations from which they could have derived strength. Instead, like the DKs, they founded record companies. This is how all of their leftist discourses eventually boiled down to a confused critique of the culture industry in which questions of autonomy, independence, and music distribution became the order of the day instead of questions about the excesses of wealth and the persistence of poverty. It is this bankrupt radicalism that led us to inflate the cultural significance of rock bands like Nirvana to such a ridiculous degree.

In the nineties, we were thereby saddled with the sinking feeling that we were witnessing something that had been done before, and done better. And then of course came the question of where this would lead us. Suicide can sometimes seem like the only way to break the cycle. The task ahead of us is to make sure that it remains a metaphor. *Maximum Rock and Roll's* original sell-out accusations in the early nineties anticipated this possibility. Unfortunately, the publication's reluctant tastemakers never moved on to the next stage of grieving, where they could start reflecting on why their illusions were shattered in the first place. This has either been left to others or wholly ignored, so that we can watch the entire cycle repeat itself until we get another Nirvana, another Dylan, or another Sex Pistols. But for now, we're in a downtime where we aren't actively searching for new heroes to magically transform our frustrated political ambitions into useless cultural capital.

❖

One aspect of the independent music community that has been explored least is its labor practices. As I've tried to show here, throughout the 1990s the alternative-culture industry was deceived by its own sales hype, believing that it had become the last vehicle for revolution in a post-political society. This is still the official ideology that drives the economics of punk and many otherwise independent countercultures. Like the propaganda of a totalitarian state, punk ideology masks a complex form of coercion. No matter how much resistance to the status quo this ideology promises, alternative artists and laborers have never been able to create work for themselves that transcends traditional forms of exploitation in a capitalist society. More often than not, bands never get paid, and the people who work at independent record labels and magazines rarely receive wages that correspond to the amount of time they invest in their jobs. With few exceptions, alternative labor is rewarded with minuscule compensation. There's absolutely nothing liberating about this, except the degree to which it shows how "the system" consistently promotes the illusion that it's possible to engage in non-exploitative labor practices in a market economy. But given the period of economic development in which we live, the power of the ideology behind alternative cultural production makes a lot of sense. It is perfectly suited to a service economy in which young people rarely spend more than a few years at any job.

Critics like Tom Frank of *The Baffler* have done a thorough job of alerting us to the ways in which alternative culture depends on the belief that it is possible to be liberated from the market through consuming the right goods. But this culture depends just as heavily on the belief that *producing* those goods is similarly liberating. Unfortunately, since many of the best critics have come from within that culture, the issue of production has been a notable blindspot. For all of its allure, the DIY ("do-it-yourself") ethic fetishizes the capitalist production process, leading people to think that one form of capitalist production can overthrow capitalism as a whole. Since it is not necessarily the product itself, but the independent nature of the production process that makes commodities like punk rock appealing, the ideology that sustains the production is particularly difficult to uproot.

There is no political criterion in the alternative-culture industry with which to distinguish it from the mainstream industry. On the most basic level, it has the same agenda: to make money. I don't mean to suggest that there is nothing good about the indie world. Whatever the contradictions, devotion to work that pays subsistence wages will always be a noble calling, especially in a society dominated by the principle of exchange, in which conscienceless individualism is considered the highest of virtues. However, the politics behind most alternative record labels do not correspond to those of their artists. The conflict between the Offspring and Epitaph Records is not an exception to the rule. It *is* the rule—not at the level of sentiment, but at the level of practical contradiction. Small, independent record labels sell revolution, but only to a limited degree; if they went whole-hog, they'd have to pay their employees better, making their enterprise unsustainable.

The sub-standard wages that pervade the business are understandable when you consider how few venues in American civil society offer the sophisticated political information and ideological perspectives of punk rock. Many of the people who work at radical indie labels do so because they identify with that need to spread the message, knowing that no one else will make it available if they don't. In this respect, they are no different from the over-educated and under-paid individuals who work at museums and galleries in the service of art.

But the utopianism and good will of these people gets exploited. The ongoing state of emergency which punk addresses serves as an implicit justification for many labels to take advantage of the willingness of their employees and bands to overextend themselves in pursuit of the right cause. Part-time employees usually work full-time. A great deal of the grunt work—packaging records for mail order, calling radio stations to track the progress of new releases, performing basic accounting chores, and maintaining complex, graphically dense promotional websites—is oftentimes carried out by unpaid interns hoping to learn skills that will eventually get them part-time paying jobs with full-time responsibilities. Is it only the illusive dream of revolution that attracts legions of young people to work that is in conflict with their own best interests? What keeps them there?

There are several explanations. To begin with, most people in the punk-rock business believe that the cycle will end. They honestly think that there will come a time when the books will begin to balance and they will be able to live off of the benefits of their labor. This makes a certain amount of sense, because in many other industries, if you work hard you'll eventually see some gain. This is also the heart of the Protestant ethic: the belief that hard work is always rewarded. It can't be underestimated how much this uniquely Christian belief system stokes the flames of labor in every exploitative employment situation in American society, punk or otherwise. As an alternative, punk offers up the DIY ethic, which in many respects is a restatement of a conservative and traditional theory of labor.

Through the impoverished models of fulfillment and self-realization that are embodied by these individuals, bands, and record companies, a certain degree of cultural capital accrues. The more successful players in this world have the satisfaction of beating popular culture at its own exploitative game. That's one of the big payoffs. There are also less cynical explanations for why hipsters sacrifice themselves to alternative capitalism so readily, such as the moral rewards of perpetuating a culture of resistance. It doesn't matter that it is only resistant to popular culture. In a society in which few acts of labor allow us to retain any sense of dignity, the conviction that one is doing something meaningful can feel truly liberating.

But for every person who gets such a job, many don't. The market's natural selection makes sure of that. Nevertheless, the culture of resistance can make living in an unjust society more tolerable. It is an opiate. That's why we sacrifice ourselves to petite-bourgeois corporations like independent record labels, whether it be in the capacity of a fan, musician, zine editor, or promoter. Eventually, we discover that our own revolutionary rationale simply becomes another strategy by which to seek upward mobility. This is what implicates us in an economic system that makes no distinctions between alternative and predominant, mainstream and independent.

We must continue to challenge our own assumptions, and appreciate how we get co-opted by the market's laws of labor that marginalize people within alternative economic formations in the same way they do outside of them. Trapped in the jaws of the market, we need a religion to console ourselves. And our religion is culture. This means that we are always searching for salvation on the inside, rather than working to build a tangibly better world.

Up until this point, I've provided a fairly negative assessment of punk's legacy. As disappointed as I have been in the ideological blindness of people in the independent music community, however, it remains *my* community. It's where I come from, just as surely as I come from Israel or the Pacific Northwest. For all my reservations about what the ideology of punk has led to in practice, I remain committed to its idealism. Even as I decry the shortcomings of its DIY ideals, I continue to do all sorts of things by myself, and for minuscule pay. That's why I want to close my discussion of music with personal reflections on a more positive note.

I almost gave up making music two years ago. There was something about it that I just couldn't connect to anymore. I used to think it was related to these negative experiences on the business side of things. Working for record companies and college radio stations was disenchanting. But founding and working on my own label was a hell of a lot more exhausting. After having taken on everything from distribution to publicity—in addition to working as a magazine editor, journalist, and doctoral student—I became convinced that my inability to write new songs was a product of being overextended.

However, my need to express myself artistically has always found its most natural vehicle in music. Ultimately, I realized that there was a problem with the very nature of the material I had always worked with: spoken word text culled from Christian radio programming. Being a Marxist, a Jew, and a satirist, I've always been seduced by religious radio's rationalization of human suffering. Together with my bandmates, I developed a musical oeuvre by creating the audio equivalent of monographs about this radio culture—punk rock without the drums, bass, and guitar. Year in and year out, for almost an entire decade, I excavated the detritus of third-rate religious programming to make a new type of protest music, one which distinguished itself not on the basis of polemics or didacticism, but through documentary recordings.

Over the course of three albums and three singles under the name the "Christal Methodists," my bandmates and I reasserted the ideological necessity of traditional leftist criticism of religion within the context of the new sampling and collage musical culture that came of age during the rise of electronica, hip hop, and techno dance music during the 1990s. And I retained my ties to the world of punk, even as I ceased listening to traditional punk records. Although my only significant engagement with rock culture during this period was my crank-call project ridiculing the bandwagon-hopping Nirvana-ites, I continued thinking in the language of punk throughout my years as a "Methodista."

I had the perfect alibi with which to promote our work without making us come across as careerists: Our band's music was designed to raise people's consciousness about how religion uses technology to further mystify devotees' experience of political disenfranchisement. Within a seven-year period, we'd been written about in nearly every major underground music magazine in North America, not to mention that we received regular airplay on a handful of American and Canadian college radio stations. We'd even had our second album, *New World Odour,* bootlegged by a label in Europe, which by my own estimates sold better than any of our releases in the US. By the time we broke up, even *Details* magazine had run a feature on us. After this ineffectual flirtation with the mainstream, I decided to call it quits. I knew this group would never amount to anything: The Christal Methodists had gotten as far as we were likely to go. We might get some more good reviews, but we were never going to reach a wider audience.

When we finished our third album, *Satanic Ritual Abuse*, I was starting to feel constrained by the source material we were working with. There was something about it that was deadening. I recorded one conversation in which a woman who'd been raped by a man she'd met at Bible study asked a radio minister if she had the right to litigate against this man for his actions, or whether she should defer to God's judgment. The clergyman, of course, replied that she should leave it in the Lord's hands and move on with her life. Such recordings were easy to work with. Just make a few edits, and build a piece of music around it. Other spoken word pieces I employed had meanings that were less obvious, requiring a certain degree of excavation. For every iconoclastic three-minute excerpt I would end up using, however, I'd spend at least a week listening to Christian talk radio, with my finger always ready to hit the record button. I don't know how I put up with it for so long, but after seven years of doing this, I finally lost my patience. I gave up. I stopped listening to Christian radio altogether.

Perhaps I was sick of hearing such horrible stories all the time. One evening as I was eating dinner, I listened to a woman on the radio describe how she'd finally figured out why she had given birth to a Down's-syndrome child: God did not favor her. I nearly choked when the radio minister cheerily agreed with her. Or perhaps I had simply completed my musical mission. Any more work with such material would be tantamount to exploiting people's tragedies, I reasoned.

Such radio programming succeeds in drawing vast audiences because the never-ending tales of devastation help numb listeners to the pain in their own lives—especially since most people who listen to such programming never experience a quarter of the difficulties that they hear about on the radio. The broadcasts tell them that their own, very real difficulties are negligible compared to what other, less fortunate people have to go through.

At a certain moment, I noticed that I was becoming one of those numbed listeners. Stuck in traffic on the way home from work one day, I found myself completely unaffected by three consecutive stories about women who had died from botched abortions. I simply accepted them in the same way that I would any other news. It was only later, when I realized that I hadn't bothered to pull out the tape recorder that I always carried with me to record such events, that it sunk in. Fundamentalism wasn't making me angry anymore. And I was starting to react to its media manifestations in the way that I criticized its faith-community adherents for reacting to it. I got scared.

I resolved to take a break. I was becoming immune to the very propaganda that I had consistently sought out in order to raise other people's consciousness of suffering. This made me question my own political priorities. I asked myself whether or not I still thought fundamentalism was a threat to democracy, and whether I was still committed to the so-called radical cause. Finally, I had to stop myself. What nonsense! Of course I was. Then what was my new lack of sensitivity all about? To put it simply: over-exposure.

Some time after abandoning this project, I discovered that I had misunderstood the centrality of artistic practices to the rest of my life. All of my other work flowed from it; my need to make music is rooted in my own life instincts, my resistance to what I've always discerned as metaphorical forces of death. In order to recognize this, I had to get to the point where both my life and death instincts became indistinguishable, because every authentic struggle for social justice carries with it the knowledge that illuminating the suffering of others involves losing oneself in both life and death instincts. Anything less than total identification leads to work which may be empathic, but is less than genuine, if not outright trite—perennially sympathetic but unable to articulate what it must be like to be truly fucked. This was what had always distinguished the Christal Methodists' work from more traditional protest music, with its slogans, hyperbole, and top-down pedagogy. The strength of our music lay in its reproduction of the actual conditions of oppression, which might therefore inspire others to appreciate what really needs changing.

All of this inner turmoil came to a head late one evening as I prepared for a trip the next day to visit the owner of our new record company in Seattle. Our third record was about to be released to the public, a full six months after we had recorded it. I felt obligated to bring a new song with me to Seattle to demonstrate that we'd already begun work on our follow-up recording.

Having spent the last several months getting absolutely nowhere, I felt desperate and apprehensive. What if I arrived without anything to show for this person's investment in our music? I paced around my room wondering what the hell I was going to do, with only eight hours before my flight and not even a pithy sample loaded into my computer.

I opened a box of CDs and vinyl that I'd brought home from a record store earlier that week. It had been payday, and concerned that I lacked the requisite source material to kick out the proverbial jams, I'd spent three hundred dollars on vintage political spoken-word recordings from the 1960s and contemporary *musique concrète* made with electric guitars. Frantically, I fingered two vinyl titles: *A GI's Tour of Germany: Documentary Sounds from the Free Side of the Berlin Wall* and *Oedipus Rex, as Performed by the Amherst College Players*.

I considered what might come of sampling Greek choruses, combining the voices of the Furies with the sounds of GIs explaining what life was like on the free-market side of the Iron Curtain. But I stopped myself; as interesting as this seemed, it would be far too much work given the time I'd allotted myself. Like a student cramming at the last minute for an important exam, my nervousness accelerated. Finally, as my anxiety reached its apotheosis, it yielded the necessary results: I pulled out *Keep The Faith, Baby*, a series of lectures by the former Harlem congressman Adam Clayton Powell Jr., bearing the seminal speech (for which the album was named) about maintaining one's dignity in the face of racism.

"That's the fucking ticket!" I shouted, as I threw the album on my turntable. Silently, I imported Powell's speech into my computer, certain that, though I hadn't listened to the sermon in years, it would suffice. Within minutes, I'd located the other sample materials I'd need for my purposes: a CD of experimental guitar noise by Sonic Youth; recordings of dueling guitar synthesizers by Chicago's Jim O'Rourke and Japanese punk guitarist KK Null; and a drum track I'd recorded several months before by my friend Luis, drummer from the queer-punk band, Pansy Division.

By the time the sun started to rise, I'd finished assembling the song. Powell's voice thundered with words of encouragement and strength; Sonic Youth's guitars, distorted and processed beyond recognition, ebbed and flowed as though commanded by the power of the orator; O'Rourke's and Null's instruments sounded like a medieval church organ filling in for an absent backing choir; and Luis's Promethean drums wrapped around Powell's beautifully articulated, inspired syllables. Delighted beyond words, I dubbed a cassette copy of the track, threw it into my bag, and drove my truck at break-neck speed to meet my departing flight in Oakland.

That same evening, after playing the foghorn in the backing band of the cantankerous, drunk British rock critic Everett True—who belted out his one and only Sub Pop single, "Do Nuts," in a thick Cockney accent to an equally inebriated crowd of Seattle's post-grunge elite—the owner of my new label accompanied my bandmate Brock and me on a ride around town, blasted, looking for a place to eat.

"Pop the tape in, Joel," Rich said. "I want to hear the new song." Proudly, I obliged.

As our car careened over the top of Capitol Hill, the drums kicked in, followed by the synths, guitars, and finally, the voice of Adam Clayton Powell. Rich's eyes opened wide, his lips parted, and he cranked up the volume. "You did it, Joel!" he yelled. "You finally wrote a song that's uplifting! Not only that, but it rocks." We looked each other in the eye, shared a healthy chuckle, and sped off to dinner.

"There's a lot more where that came from," I told him. "I'm not sure it's going to be called the Christal Methodists, but I think I found my groove again."

I had finally figured out a way to have my punk and play it, too.

Schalit family: Michael, Harriet, Elie, and Naomi, London, England, 1

MY OWN PRIVATE ISRAEL

When I was a child, I never collected toys or baseball cards. I shied away from team sports, hated disco, and never worried about how I looked. War was essentially the only thing I thought about. It started with my parents' book collection. The titles I remember them having in their library were mostly English- and Hebrew-language coffee-table books commemorating Israel's victory in the Six-Day War of 1967. Like many Israelis of their generation, they were obsessed with the conflict. It had been the first popularly recognized Jewish military victory since biblical times. And it came for a country that had very few modern weapons at its disposal at that time, a country that saw in every new Jeep that it acquired another reassurance that it wouldn't be destroyed. This was an issue that most of the propaganda books that my parents owned spent an inordinate amount of space focusing on.

For example, on one page there'd be a picture of a Mirage IIIC flying over the Sinai. A typical caption would revel in all the details of the plane's remarkable offensive characteristics, describing its payload, what kind of cannon it used, the power of its turbofans. On another page there would be a picture of a Willy's Jeep mounted with a recoilless rifle. Underneath, the caption would describe the importance of such cheap forms of mobile artillery for a country short on mortars and self-propelled artillery. Not only would such books give the reader a history of Israeli military prowess, but they would also provide an education in modern armaments. Over time, these two features fused together. The message to the new nation's citizens was clear: Our weaponry, and how we use it, is the foundation of our new national identity.

Even though this kind of literature was ubiquitous in Israel's fledgling media culture, it wasn't just propaganda. It was also emblematic of the country's anxieties about survival and its resulting fetishization of weapons of war. Everyone engaged in this projection, because everyone served in the army. When the Israel Defense Forces acquired a new weapons system, it was a momentous event for the entire country. When a weapons deal was being negotiated with the United States, everyone knew about it. You'd hear about it from children in the hallways of your elementary school or from your parents at the dinner table—even if such events had no direct impact on their lives. Everyone had an investment in the military. And it made sense: Our country was in a permanent state of war.

However understandable the emergence of this sort of culture may be, a preoccupation with instruments of violence leads people to accept them as necessary. Somehow, their importance as a tool of survival becomes too familiar. Personal valuations of weaponry should be regarded as temporary, rather than a permanent part of one's identity. This is particularly true for people living in a region engulfed in a constant state of conflict. For those who cannot remember a time without violence, it is doubly important that they not have their imaginations circumscribed by a sense of inevitability. But freeing the imagination is easier said than done. I can attest to this. I could have used more education in visualizing a different state of affairs. But I didn't get that schooling, and, as a result, I can never wholly forget the ways of making war. In this respect, I suppose you could call me a typical Israeli.

When I was ten, my father and I moved from Israel to England. I immediately fell into a state of culture shock. The English, I used to think, were wussies. They seemed so easily led around by the nose; I was sure they had never had it very hard. They were fanatical about soccer and rock and roll. I couldn't relate to English culture at all. My response was to recreate what I knew of Israel in my own head. Bookstores became quite important to me. Whenever I went into one, I found myself heading straight for the military history section. If the store lacked such a section, I would hightail it to the magazine rack and search for military-oriented periodicals. *Armies and Weapons*, *Interavia*, *Aviation Week*, and *Space Technology* were particular favorites of mine. Oversized coffee-table books about the Second World War were always a feast for my eyes, particularly those that focused on vintage tanks and fighter aircraft employed by the Allies and their foes. By the time I was twelve, I was an acknowledged expert in twentieth-century military weaponry.

A major impetus for this interest was the parental affirmation it brought me. Whenever we went back home to Israel, my father would trot me out at parties and have his retired officer friends quiz me on the latest developments in weapons technology. I'd be asked to give my opinion on the relative merits of multi-caliber infantry weapons such as the Israeli Galil, which fired both 5.56mm Russian standard cartridges as well as NATO-compatible 7.62mm munitions. "It's the ideal infantry assault rifle," I remember once telling a former general. "If you're fighting a NATO army, you can pilfer M-16 and FN cartridges from their dead and use them if you're running low on ammo. Same goes for if you're fighting an Arab army using Kalashnikovs. Just strip the corpses and voilà, no need to worry about supply lines. All sizes fit." My father's friends would be amazed. I was a very troubled child.

At a certain point, my preoccupation with all things military started to take on more serious overtones. I first became cognizant of this when I was thirteen and my father's retired air force friend Benji decided that it was time I start learning how to use those weapons I seemed to know so much about. One Saturday afternoon at a party in his palatial orange-grove home in Rishon Le Zion, Benji pulled out an AK-47, an Uzi, and an M-16, all of which he stored in his basement. "Yoel," he said, "I want you to strip these weapons bare, clean them, and put them all back together again. *Yallah, Habibi* [Get going, kid], you've got two hours to figure it out."

What I remember most vividly about that moment is the terror I felt inside. I wondered if I was about to be discovered as a fraud. Here I was, for the first time staring down the empty barrels of my fixation. I did not have the slightest idea what to do. Everything else from there on in remains a metaphorical "blank," except for my father and Benji congratulating me for thinking so quickly on my feet. Without the benefit of written instructions or legible English-language manuals, I had completed the task. "He'll make a fine officer," Benji remarked with a huge smile on his face, congratulating my father with a warm slap on the back. "Elie, the future of *Zahal* [the Israeli Army] lies in the hands of our children. Your son is as much a testimony to this as any commando I've seen."

My father turned red with pride, his eyes lighting up like cedar-tree decorations in Bethlehem at Christmas. *"Nu Benji,"* Elie replied. "We'll have to reserve a spot for Yoel in officer's training school as soon as he is eligible."

I breathed a huge sigh of relief. *I guess I'm not such a poseur after all*, I thought. *Maybe I'll get an extra piece of baklava.* That was really all I cared about. Considering everything my father and his friends

IDF Armoured Corps Museum, Latrun, Israel, 1998

were investing in my activities, a creeping sense of doubt about my own motivations for being such a *chacham*—or "know-it-all"—when it came to matters of killing started to worry me. If the only reward I was seeking was an extra piece of baklava, there was obviously something wrong with my soul. I carried this feeling of guilt around for quite some time, as I knew I had no overriding moral objection to what I was doing.

Over time, I began to lose interest in weapons. And I realized that I was lying to everyone because I didn't want to lose their approval. While I became more internally disconnected from my hobby, my father and his friends became more obsessed with it. Wherever we went, my legend among middle-aged military officers and politicians seemed to follow. During a lunch meeting at a Moroccan restaurant in Jerusalem not long after he had first left office, Yitzhak Rabin gave me a model F-4 Phantom jet for my birthday. I sat quietly, staring at my couscous, thinking, *Rabin gave me a Phantom jet, Rabin gave me a Phantom jet . . .* A year or so later, Jerusalem's former mayor Teddy Kollek gave me the exact same gift at the exact same restaurant. As flattered as I was at the attention being bestowed upon me by my father's old friends, I started to fear that I would have to live up to my reputation some day.

Sensing there was something potentially destructive about my looming self-doubt—I kept having visions of grenades exploding in an empty Jerusalem square—I bottled it up inside me. What would happen if my father found out? What would he do if the basis for all of his friends' appreciation of me was undermined? I would not only be letting my father down in public, but I might also do irreparable harm to what had become a very close relationship between father and son—one built almost exclusively on war.

But time, not to mention adolescence, eventually began to take its toll. One humid day in the summer of 1979, wandering the streets of Lugano, Switzerland, out of money, looking for something to do, my father and I stumbled upon a movie theater showing the latest American hit, *The Deerhunter.* Elie spent our last bit of cash on two tickets. By the end of the film, he was in tears. I sat there in a complete state of shock.

As we walked out, my father reflected on the scene in which Robert De Niro, egged on by his Viet Cong captors, undertakes a game of Russian Roulette. Christopher Walken dies. For the first time, my father talked about having been a prisoner of war, first incarcerated by the British along with Rabin in the late 1930s, and later by the Syrians in a military stockade in Damascus, from which he escaped after six months of near-starvation. I had never heard my father speak so somberly of what it meant to be at war. It came as a total revelation, providing justification for my discomfort at being a trained pseudo-Israeli parakeet reeling off weapons statistics. Out of money, we wandered to the waterfront. Little did I know how much further my father would go in disabusing me of my waning fetish.

Staring out at the lights on the other side of Lake Como, Elie roundly condemned my fascination with all things military. "Can't you find other things to think about, Yoel?" he asked. "Can't you devote yourself to other interests, like sports or girls, the way other young children do?"

I didn't know what to say. I had spent the last few years finding ways to please him, not only because I thought I was following in his footsteps as a soldier, but also because Israel, in the form of my father's friends, required this of me. Somehow, if I were able to be educated about the ways and means of warfare, despite my increasing misgivings, I would be both a model son and a model citizen. We stood there in silence, while the sounds of Kiss' "I Was Made For Loving You" blasted out of the speakers of an open-air discotheque in the distance. I could see beads of sweat rolling down my father's balding, wrinkled forehead. *You look old,* I thought. *So old, I almost don't know you. There's something missing in your eyes. They seem blank, almost vacant, and yet the only thing behind them are tears.* I began to tremble slightly.

Suddenly, this man, my father, was a stranger to me. I spent the next twenty years of my life unable to decipher what that empty stare of his meant. That is, until one day last year when a videocassette arrived in the mail. It was an interview with my father for Israeli television. My roommate Annalee and I immediately put it on and began watching. "Your father has the longest thousand-yard stare I've ever seen," Annalee remarked. Two decades of puzzlement seemed to collapse in a matter of seconds. I excused myself and stepped out onto our back porch to have a cigarette and calm down. Peering down on our filthy backyard full of wet laundry blowing in the lukewarm spring wind, I realized why my father's empty stare troubled me so twenty years before. He'd seen enough death to last a thousand lifetimes. Even though I knew that intellectually, I'd never fully acknowledged how his body had been changed by it. I started to cry.

Later that afternoon, unable to concentrate, I quit my schoolwork and drove my truck down to the beach. It was still early enough that barely a soul was present, except for a stray woman walking a dog. The only sound was the hum of traffic moving up and down the highway. Clouds hovered over the water. I imagined myself a ship heading west, so far west that I was crossing the Indian Ocean, viewing the faint outline of the coast of Yemen, about to enter the Red Sea, destined for a port somewhere along the Suez Canal. My daydreaming was suddenly interrupted by a sonic boom. I looked up and saw the fuselages of a team of dark-blue, dual-finned fighter planes, which I identified immediately. They were US Navy F-18s from the Blue Angels acrobatic team on their annual visit to San Francisco. An oddly reassuring feeling overcame me. It was okay to know what kind of aircraft they were. I turned around and watched the fighters until I couldn't see them anymore.

I remembered when my family moved to a house in the Tel Aviv suburb of Savyon that we rented from an Iranian acquaintance. Awoken by a series of extremely loud sonic booms our first morning there, I rushed into my father's room, yelling, "Abba, Abba, what's going on? Are we at war again?"

"No, child," he replied. "We live next to an airport now. Those are our new American fighter planes, the best ones in the world."

"What model are they?" I asked excitedly.

"The F-15 Eagle. It's a dual-finned fighter bomber that can fly all the way to Cairo and back with a full complement of air-to-surface weapons, if necessary."

Years later, my girlfriend and I were standing in the Miami office of my now-deceased older brother Michael, an ex-paratrooper. We were stopping over briefly for the two of them to meet each other en route to Israel to visit my parents. As we waited for Michael to get off the phone, I looked over at his bookshelf and saw several coffee-table volumes about the history of the Israel Defense

Forces, along with several editions of *Jane's* annual weapons guides. Bored, and anxious to get on with our trip, I pulled them out and began showing them to Cori. "There was a point in my life when I could tell you anything you wanted to know about modern weaponry," I said. "The scary thing is that I can still remember most of it. See, those are remodeled Shermans from the Second World War sporting new turrets and 75mm guns." Cori looked amused.

Half-listening to our conversation, Michael cupped his hand over the telephone, smiled, and said, "When we were children, that was required knowledge. It never leaves you."

As Cori and I boarded the plane to Tel Aviv, I thought hard about the truth in Michael's words. I knew that as soon as we got to Israel, I'd end up unconsciously taking inventory of the weapons soldiers were carrying on the street. It still made me feel uneasy. *Why can't I lose my knowledge?* I wondered as our plane left the ground. Then I recalled my last trip to Miami. Michael had insisted we go shooting. "No, man, I don't want to do that," I had told him. "Can't we go to an aquarium or do something a little more benign?" Michael refused to answer.

I then remember driving with Michael straight to the shooting range, two rifles and several hundred rounds of ammo in tow. When we arrived, twenty or so Cubans in camouflage uniforms and baseball hats wearing large headphones were firing away. I was deafened by the roar. I started cataloguing the assault rifles—old American M-1s, German Heckler and Koch G3s, Israeli Uzis and Galils, AR-15s, M-16s, AK-47s of a variety of different national brands, even Mac 10s. It was overwhelming. Then, of course, it was my turn to join in. Michael handed me a fully loaded Chinese-made Kalashnikov. "All you have to do is look straight through the site, Joel. The target should be right there, down the middle. Just squeeze the trigger and FIRE."

Horrified by the task at hand, I picked up the rifle and slid the butt into my armpit. For some reason, it felt natural. "Good, Joel, good. You know exactly what you're doing," Michael said, trying to be encouraging. Truth was, my heart was pounding; my ears felt hot; sweat was pouring down my forehead. Finally, I said fuck it, and I took aim and fired. Once I had finished, we both looked at the target. Not a single bullet of mine had hit it. Taking stock of the results, Michael turned to me with a grin and said rather affectionately, "Joel, let's face it, you'll never make a good sniper."

I'm glad I won't make a good sniper. As powerful as the pull of my heritage may be, there's still hope that I can be reprogrammed. The hard part is figuring out a way to do this without losing touch with the past. When members of a cult undergo ideological deconditioning, their membership often becomes a blank. And it takes on new power as a result. I want something different for myself and all Israelis. We need to remember the pain of the past without indulging the reflexes it has instilled in us.

This is a huge challenge, particularly when you come from a family with a history like my own. The point was driven home to me during the trip with Cori through Israel's northernmost territory. (My parents live in a well-to-do beach town located halfway between Tel Aviv and Haifa, appropriately named Caesarea.) We had traveled to Israel (via Miami) after spending Christmas with Cori's family in Davis, California. Everything had gone marvelously there. It was the first time I'd ever experienced a happy Christmas with a family that didn't make me feel alienated for being Jewish. Granted, Cori's family is not the least bit religious. Her mother comes from a Protestant background, her stepfather a Jewish one, and her sister-in-law is a secular Bengali. The combination of cultures and personalities involved was part of what made it the first Christmas in two decades of living in America that felt inclusive. But most powerful was being so deeply in love. I couldn't have asked for a better set of circumstances. I was on top of the world.

Unfortunately, Israel has a way of reminding me how illusory such fleeting experiences of euphoria can be. A feeling of estrangement was driven home hard our first full day in the so-called Holy Land. Eager to show Cori my favorite parts of the region, I decided to take her on a trip and wind our way to the Golan Heights. "You've never seen anything like it," I told her. "It's absolutely stunning. And we're about to give it back to the Syrians." Soon enough, we were en route in my father's '89 Peugeot, stopping for bottled water at a gas station on the outskirts of the working-class immigrant town of Hadera.

Then, as we began our ascent into Wadi Ara, driving through a corridor of Arab villages, I noticed in my rearview mirror that an aging VW Rabbit was playing chicken with us. I tried to get out of its way, but the car kept tailing us. We started to get nervous. Whenever I switched lanes, so did the VW. And it was moving closer. Fearing we were going to get rammed, I slowed down to let the car pass. Instead, it pulled right alongside us, and the driver and I looked one another in the eye.

"Asshole!" I yelled, giving him a very visible middle finger. Our harasser kindly responded by flashing a pocketknife, screaming something. As I vainly attempted to drop behind him, I saw that the interior of his car was very elegantly decorated in a way that Jewish-owned cars just aren't. My heart sank. Catching on to my evasive moves, he decelerated, too. A car chase was on, between us—a shaved-bald Jew on vacation with his tattooed-and-pierced American girlfriend—and an enraged Israeli Arab behind the wheel of a rusting German car.

I immediately gunned the accelerator, but our potential assailant remained directly behind us. Frightened, I gripped the wheel so tightly my knuckles turned white. I prayed that we'd lose our friend before we reached the Israeli military police station full of heavily armed border troops on the other side of the mountain range. Lord knows what would happen. Despite my ambivalence toward them, I knew I might have no choice about seeking their assistance.

We suddenly reached a four-way intersection with one direction leading to Um Al-Fahm, a village of 40,000 residents, once the bastion of Israel's Communist Party, now one of the centers of the country's burgeoning Islamic movement. The Israeli army had ignited riots the year before by confiscating Arab-owned orchards for use as a new firing range. I wondered if the man chasing us came from there. I looked in my rearview mirror and saw the VW making a sharp right turn into town. Fearful that this was a ruse, I continued to accelerate until we passed the military police station and descended into the Valley of Jezre'el, where, according to the Book of Revelations, Armageddon was supposed to take place the very next day. As biblical fate would have it, doomsday would not arrive before its designated time. We were no longer being chased by a knife-wielding Muslim. (Eight months later, on the morning of October 1, 2000, following a prayer service and funeral procession for four Palestinians shot to death by Israeli police in Jerusalem, Israeli security forces, including snipers, fired on a crowd of demonstrators blocking that same intersection, killing three people and injuring sixty more.)

This incident cast a pall over the rest of our vacation. And the vacation, in turn, cast a pall over our burgeoning romance. But it did offer me a new perspective on my relationship with Israel. A little later in the trip, we were standing on the ramparts of the crusader fortress in Acre. Wherever I am in the country, my thoughts usually turn to my family. But, for once, I was thinking about something else. The town mullahs had started to issue their evening call to prayer. Within seconds of one another, the two minarets within view began their broadcast in the most melancholy of reverbs, the kind that any haute couture American sound engineer would die for. Gazing out at the Mediterranean, I clasped Cori's hand, bathing in the sound-delay created by the dueling muezzins. Their calls to piety sounded like a high-speed chase to holiness through the stinking, serpentine alleyways below us, taking hold of this testament to ancient European colonialism, making it Arab again.

For as long as I could remember, I had considered Acre a French city. It had been named after St. Jean D'Acre by the Crusaders, who ruled the town between 1104 and 1291, when it was captured by the Mamluk Sultan, al-Ashraf Khalil. In 1799, Napoleon's forces laid siege to it, as did the Haganah's Carmeli Brigade a century and a half later in 1948, seizing the typhoid-struck city filled with refugees fleeing Haifa as well as many smaller villages to the south. During my childhood, whenever my father took me to this town at the north end of Haifa Bay, he'd always remind me of these facts. Acre's architecture was blatantly Arab, from its famous citadel and its Great Mosque of Al Jazzar, to the bazaar beneath us. The town had remained predominantly under Muslim rule until the British conquered the northern half of Palestine in the fall of 1918. But since Acre's namesake was a Christian saint, it was marked as foreign in my mind. It gave the town the strange aura of being under continuous occupation, a monument to the effects of European colonialism. Since 1948, of course, the colonizers have been European Jews returning "home" to displace the natives. The irony is almost too much to bear.

I stared at the rooftops of the ancient city and my thoughts returned, inevitably, to my family. I wondered where I might find the prison where my father had been held as a teenager in the mid-1930s. I'd promised myself that I'd seek out the old icon of British imperial rule, where he spent several months doing hard labor shuffling books in the prison library as punishment for getting caught on the beach near Haifa smuggling in Jewish refugees. But in the end, I decided not to look for it. And I couldn't figure out what was stopping me. Nervous about the trip home, I postponed trying to answer this question and got us back on the road to Haifa. Something about Acre was making me uneasy.

An hour later, Cori and I passed through downtown Haifa in the darkness and contemplated stopping at the long line of Arab fast-food joints that straddle the road. Their glowing neon lights, filthy floors, and huge racks of roasting shwarma rotating on vertical, heated skewers were familiar to me, just like the soldiers usually standing outside of them eating falafel out of small paper bags, tahina dripping onto the ends of their rifle butts. This was the Israel I first knew as a child, defined by its Middle Eastern food, rounded out by its army, simultaneously Arab and European. Tonight, however, there were no soldiers, just a few Israeli Arabs milling around, looking restless. Not a good time to stop, I sensed.

I'd never spent much time in this part of northern Israel. My strongest memory of the region was the day my father drove us up to Rosh Hanikra, on the Lebanese border. It was 1975 and I was eight years old. The Lebanese civil war had just begun. From an outpost along the frontier, we watched Christian and Muslim militiamen trade artillery fire. The exchange came so close that the ground shook underneath our feet. I distinctly recall my father taking out his binoculars to get a closer look at what the Lebanese were firing at each other.

"Mortars, Katyushas," he had said, referring to what remains the most common form of guerilla weaponry in the Middle East—lightweight artillery pieces, the former firing a spring-loaded shell, the latter a small-caliber, inexpensive, truck-mounted rocket infamous for its lack of accuracy. "They're tearing each other apart, those poor bastards," he added.

This was the first weekend after we'd moved to Israel. My mother had died two months before, and my father thought it would be best to bring me home from America and raise me in a place where he had enough family members to help out. Besides, Israel was the mother of us all. With Mom gone, who better to replace her with than the biggest family ever—not just the "Schalitim," as we've always called ourselves, but the country my father had helped breathe life into. I remember driving back to Tel Aviv that night as a young boy thinking that I'd arrived in a really warm and exciting country.

I wanted to watch the Lebanese shoot at each other again, but my father had the good sense never to take me back. He'd witnessed violence at the same age, during the Arab riots that raged throughout Palestine in 1929. After that first experience of violence, he was never able to break free of its grip.

Beginning with his stint as a teenage member of the underground, the Haganah—well before the establishment of the Israeli state—my father, a native Israeli, had spent most of his life in the military, remaining active in the reserves into his sixties. I've always considered him lucky in this regard. Not because of the risks such an existence entailed. He made it clear that he abhorred violence, insisting that it should only be used as a last resort. I envied not what my father had done, but the conviction with which he had done it: his belief in a Jewish state. As an eight-year-old, I was grateful for the existence of that state. In light of the destruction that I had witnessed firsthand from our safe haven at the border, Israel seemed like an ocean of calm next to the anarchy of Lebanon. It was a refuge from the dark history of our people's time in Europe, from the concentrations camps back to the pogroms and Inquisitions before them. And, most importantly, it was not America. The United States had become a place of death for me with my mother's premature passing. Israel, by contrast, held the promise of a new life.

This is where my fixation with war was born. Before I was trying to impress my father's friends, I was a soldier battling the pain of an unspeakable loss. If Israel could muster the will to survive, so could I. I rebelled against an America that had betrayed me by mimicking my father's soldierly ways. The helicopters flying overhead all day, the soldiers on the streets, and the sonic booms of fighter-bombers that shook our house every morning were signifiers of strength I found too compelling to ignore.

Despite his pride at my burgeoning mastery of weaponry, my father always tried to impose limits on how the symbolism of warfare empowered me. Whenever he could, he'd drive me through the Occupied Territories and talk about how much he admired Arabs, with their rich histories and non-European cultures. Often, we'd visit Palestinian acquaintances, with whom he spoke gorgeous, fluent Arabic, sipping café Turkie, politely puffing on the tobacco in their pipes over mint tea. My father relished these trips, as though they gave him access to a Middle Eastern identity that was more authentically Jewish than the one our family had brought from Europe in the early 1880s.

This was the other side of my father's Israeli identity, the one that wasn't warlike. It represented the dream of "going native" with the region's Arab inhabitants instead of fighting against them. I identified with my father's neighborliness as much as his warrior self, particularly as I grew older and started to become disenchanted with all the violence and killing. But I wasn't very in touch with this sentiment until Israel invaded Lebanon in 1982 and I found myself profoundly disgusted by all of the civilian casualties incurred in pursuit of a solution to the threat that the Palestinians posed to Israel's northern border.

I couldn't help but see my father's Palestinian acquaintances in the nightly body counts on television, facsimiles of their homes underneath the treads of our tanks and armored personnel carriers.

"Sharon's War," as many Israelis called it, was the first conflict in which I personally felt that we had transgressed my father's moral boundaries regarding the use of violence. This experience utterly transformed me. Watching the media images of tanks rolling over houses in Sidon, Tyre, the Beka'a Valley, and Beirut, I became convinced that there were no more just wars to be fought on behalf of the Jewish state. Four years later, when it came time for me to serve in the army, I quietly refused, choosing instead to stay in Portland and enroll in a college to study religion. Better to be an American, I thought—in an about-face to my previous revulsion toward the country—regardless of all the ugly contradictions. Better to study Israel from afar, through the pages of *The Oregonian* and the *New York Times*, than to be a not-so-nice Jewish boy in a uniform.

I spent the next ten years of my life trying to justify my decision. I needed to find something uniquely Israeli about myself, even though I'd evaded my military service by remaining in America. When Ehud Barak was elected prime minister in 1999, I began to entertain thoughts about going back; it seemed as though the country might actually be changing. The scent of peace was in the air. After seventeen years of occupation, the army had finally withdrawn from Lebanon, and there was even talk of sharing Jerusalem. This could indeed become the Israel of my father's dreams.

In retrospect, I should have recognized how much work still needed to be done before real change could take place. At the time, flush with my renewed national pride, I was blindsided by the implosion of the dream. Likud leader Ariel Sharon's visit to the Haram Al-Sharif on September 28, 2000 seemed to undo years of progress overnight. As I read the accounts of the uprising which began the next day, and the combat between the army and the Palestinians in the weeks that followed, it felt as though I'd been transported back in time. Not just to the period immediately preceding our invasion of Lebanon, but to a stage in my development

Graffiti and garbage in an abandoned lot, Tel Aviv, Israel, 2000

when I could have permanently dehumanized Arabs instead of seeing them as potential friends.

Had Sharon's own moral imagination ever transcended that childish single-mindedness? It seemed clear that, at a certain point in his long life of fighting, he'd given in to it all and begun to see the occupation of territory "won" in war as an end unto itself. That was the only way to explain his provocative visit to one of Islam's holiest sites. Only an idiot would not have anticipated the consequences of this move. And Sharon, whatever else you want to call him, is not an idiot. The visit to the Haram Al-Sharif was his calculated play to rule from below, to subvert the peace process without being prime minister, and, ironically, to cooperate with the extremists on the Palestinian side who saw no value in a comprehensive settlement.

Watching the footage of the corpse of a captured Israeli reservist being thrown out of the window of the police station in Ramallah, I found myself reliving the tension I had experienced on that trip to Acre several months before. Every gunshot broadcast on the news brought me back to that sense that everything was about to descend into barbarism once again. It's what stopped me from getting out of my car in places where, unlike Sharon, I felt I did not belong, such as the stretch of road I'd been harassed on, leading back to my parents' home near Hadera.

That night, as Cori and I passed a series of Arab villages that separated the highway from the sea, I pondered the discomfort I had felt at the prospect of staying in Acre after dark. Maybe the fascination of witnessing the artillery exchange nearly twenty-five years earlier had subconsciously returned to me while we were in Acre—especially given the fact that I had avoided visiting the prison where my father had been interred as a teenager. The two were indeed connected, I reasoned. I had avoided visiting the prison because I did not want to be confronted with the institutionalization of any kind of guilt. The presence of a prison in Israel, in a historically Arab community, so close to the place where I first witnessed war and found that I liked it, made me positively ill.

Throughout our entire trip, I found myself vainly seeking out locations in the country that would testify to a more clear-cut state of affairs, where I wouldn't have any sense of personal responsibility for the unequal distribution of ethnic power that is Israel. When we finally arrived in the Golan Heights, which Israel seized in the 1967 Six-Day War, I explained to Cori that this might be the last time she would get to see this gorgeous, sad plateau, since we were slated to give it back to the Syrians. And rightly so. After thirty-three years of occupation, it was still Syrian territory. As it appeared to many members of the peace camp at the time, there would be no peace with

Syria unless we returned it to them. Yet I could hear ambivalence in my own voice. Regardless of the contempt and rage I felt toward those narrow-minded, stupid Israelis who would rather commit the country to war again than return this territory to Syria, I recognized what made them prefer the death of their own children to the surrender of this strategically crucial piece of real estate.

Giving back the Golan was more significant than merely exchanging land for peace. It would also mean trading in the only military conquest that Israelis can claim in good conscience, the only one that didn't create a shadow-state of eternally displaced persons. Factor in Syria's status as a Middle-Eastern North Korea—a brutally repressive police state run by a minority Muslim warrior caste living off the exportation of terrorism and heroin, maintaining its own army of occupation in Lebanon—and you have Israel's only clear-cut strategic foil to distinguish itself from its enemies, to prove that Zionism isn't so bad after all. Considering that Israel has become equally stigmatized, one can easily imagine the lost innocence wrapped up in that landscape. And that's precisely why we will eventually have to get rid of the Golan: to remove the last meaningful alibi and absolve ourselves of our responsibility for the Palestinian dilemma.

I felt the push and pull of this insight as we stood on the side of the road, looking out over the Vale of Tears. In the 1973 Yom Kippur War, this was the site of one of the largest tank battles in world history. Hundreds of Israeli and Syrian tanks fired at each other at point-blank range, oftentimes passing within several feet of one another. Staring across the gentle slopes of the hills surrounding the Vale, one can imagine how freely the blood flowed in this alpine graveyard, and how much the scent of death can arouse the most primal combative instincts in people who truly feel themselves to be under the gun. Surveying the carefully arranged rusting wreckage of old Russian armored vehicles, I had the impression that something about this land had been sacrificed for everyone to claim ownership of it. I don't mean ownership in the ordinary sense. I'm referring to the sense of possession created by the peak experiences of human misery that people encounter during wartime, the sort that reveal the horror underpinning all borders and national identities. Ideally, the heightened consciousness of wartime would inspire the desire for collective ownership of world real estate. Unfortunately, the opposite usually occurs. Even as people on both sides of a conflict recognize that a battleground transcends the reasons for the battle, they refuse to share it. War instills in people a sense of sacrifice. That not only makes it nearly impossible for people to share with those whom they perceive to be different, but it also turns them into victims seeking to inflict the shame and trauma of displacement onto others.

As we continued our drive around the Golan, I pointed out the Druze village of Majdal Shams, thinking that we might want to stop there to grab a bite to eat before descending the northern side of the plateau. "There's nothing like Druze kubbeh," I told Cori, ignoring the Syrian flags which local villagers had raised over their homes to protest the Israeli occupation. "The way the ground beef and pine nuts are wrapped in a deep fried, cracked-wheat shell is perhaps the greatest testament to the culinary genius of the Middle East," I joked, half-serious, half-hungry. But we didn't stop.

Cori's eerily silent face looked disgusted. She was gazing at the half-complete, empty buildings, rusting agricultural machinery, and garbage spread all over the sides of the road. "Just look at how fucked up this all is," she said.

"I can't make any excuses for this," I replied.

She looked at me in a state of shock. I knew exactly what she was thinking: *Why would he even think of stopping here?* I desperately hoped that she'd forgive me. Not just for this awkward moment, but for all the others we'd experienced on the trip. I quickly asked her for a piece of pita with hummus. She generously complied.

Once again, I found myself passing everything by, eager to return home to forget the experience of contradiction. I sped down the Golan toward Banyas, where there were some pretty springs and the ruins of another old Crusader fortress nearby, the slopes of Lebanon within immediate view. I hoped I might find a moment in this day where I could enjoy being in Israel, where I could find a place so old, so far removed from the present that I could lose this inescapable sense of complicity. But by the time we arrived there, darkness had almost descended and the archaeological site was locked up.

Peering over the inaccessible ruins, listening to the water rushing underneath the rickety wooden bridge we'd crossed to get there, for the first time in years I recalled the words that my father had said nearly a quarter-century before in Nazareth. He had been paying a visit to an old Arab friend who made teak furniture engraved with mother of pearl, when a group of teenage Palestinians showered our brand new Italian sports coupe with a hail of rocks. Raising his rifle in the air, pretending that he was about to let loose a round of bullets, my father said, "Look at these children, Yoel. They're Arabs, yet they have blue eyes and a reddish tint to their hair. You know what that means? They're descended from Crusaders." Years later, he and I recalled this incident after reading an article in *Ha'aretz* about international condemnation of Israel's use of rubber bullets on Palestinian demonstrators. I asked my father whether he would have fired his rifle. "No," he emphatically stated, "I would never have done such a thing. Anyway, the magazine was empty."

When I try to make sense of the reality of my ancestral homeland, I remind myself of my father's comments about those children. His words provide a double lesson. On the one hand, they are evidence of the depth with which the legacy of European colonialism saturates the land. And, on the other hand, they reinforce the notion that nothing in Israel is as simple as one is initially inclined to believe.

❖

Early in my life, flights from the US to Israel were always crowded with Jews, military advisors, and American businessmen; there were never any Arabs in our midst. By 1998, the complexion of my fellow travelers had begun to change. Setting out on a trip to visit my family, I arrived at the Detroit airport and found the boarding area overflowing with people. In front of me stood several young Palestinian women wearing traditional *chadors* around their heads. Their small children, dressed in blue jeans and Nirvana T-shirts, milled about restlessly, as easily recognizable Israeli security agents talked into their collars, slim wires snaking up their cleanly shaven necks from underneath pressed Oxford shirts into huge, fish-belly white ears. Their young eyes scanned the Palestinians in the waiting area for potential problems.

I saw one of them staring at me and said, *"Shalom, Habibi."* Caught off guard by my Hebrew, the security agent quickly turned away. I wondered what it would be like to sit next to a Palestinian on a flight to Israel, what kind of questions they'd ask, where they'd be headed.

Several weeks earlier, I had been sitting in the back of a cab in Seattle, when I discerned by his accent that the driver might have been a Palestinian. I asked him where he was originally from, and he answered, "Yahud," an old Arab town I had lived near as a child, just outside Tel Aviv.

"I used to live in Savyon," I replied.

"Then you are my brother," he said warmly, glancing back at

me through his rearview mirror with a big, beaming smile—much like the one he inspired in me.

I remembered that moment as I waited in line at the Detroit airport. *God*, I thought to myself, *what a nice change.* Other than the visits with my dad's Palestinian friends, the only places I ever saw Arabs as a child were construction projects in Tel Aviv as migrant day laborers or on weekend trips with my father to East Jerusalem to shop for things like Persian rugs in the flea markets of the dank-smelling Old City. Traveling alongside Palestinians seemed like a sign of the progress being made in the peace negotiations between Israel and the PLO. But as I stared out at the mixed Arab-Israeli-American crowd, I wondered if I was looking at the *only* sign of progress left over from the Oslo era.

A couple of hours into the flight, the television newscaster on the video screen in front of me announced that the West Bank and the Gaza Strip had been sealed off again. Freedom of movement between the two territories through Israel had once more been frozen because a van driven by a Palestinian had exploded in the midday traffic of downtown Jerusalem. Someone had accidentally rear-ended the vehicle, setting alight a cache of gasoline, nails, and explosives that it had been carrying in preparation for a truck bombing. The driver was badly burned, but he survived. As usual, Israel blamed the PLO for not taking tight enough security measures against Muslim militant organizations. Prime Minister Binyamin "Bibi" Netanyahu told reporters that the thwarted incident demonstrated that Arafat still could not be trusted to control his own people. Peace talks were again being suspended. It was back to business as usual.

Once I'd eaten dinner, I turned on my Power Book and started reading hundreds of pages of articles that I had downloaded from Israeli and Arab newspapers on the Internet—*Ha'aretz*, the *Jordan Times*, and *Al-Ahram Weekly*. I was determined to reacquaint myself with what was going on in the region. It was the first time in years that I'd voluntarily immersed myself in Middle Eastern media. I had left Israel permanently in 1980. A trip to attend my niece's Bat Mitzvah, this was only my third visit home in eighteen years.

I eventually fell asleep. When I woke up, the plane was landing in Amsterdam, where most of us on board would catch a connecting flight to Israel. I hurriedly packed my carry-on bags and rushed into the terminal ahead of the other connecting passengers. The only thing on my mind was a cup of coffee and a cigarette. Lo and behold, I spotted an espresso stand straight ahead. I ordered a double cappuccino, a croissant, and an orange juice. Within minutes I'd consumed it all. As I fumbled through my backpack looking for my smokes, I glanced up and saw the Palestinian women I had boarded the plane with engaging in the same search. Lighting my first cigarette in eight hours, I turned toward them and we exchanged the warm smiles of fellow smokers. Several minutes later, noticing the clock, we stubbed out our butts and hurried to catch the connecting flight.

Entering a security-check zone, I approached a phalanx of Dutch soldiers armed with machine guns and hand-held computers. One of them typed my American passport information into his miniature PC and said, "Aren't you an Israeli citizen?"

"No," I lied to him. "Not any more."

He smiled and asked why.

"Because I stayed in America to attend university," I replied.

"Well, according to my records, you are still an Israeli, Mister Schlitz. Please check in with immigration when you get to Tel Aviv. You might have some problems with them." Just what I needed.

Few things inspire greater anxiety in me than passing through passport control in Tel Aviv, since I never did my army service.

Every time I go through immigration at Ben Gurion airport, my identity check goes awry and I am asked why I don't travel on my Israeli passport. I always tell them that it's not important. They look at me kind of funny and start barking in Hebrew. My policy is to always reply in English. Why not just save the pain and get an Israeli passport? Because if I came home using Israeli ID, I'd be read the riot act about draft dodging and possibly end up in the military.

As I sat half-asleep on the flight, I dreamed of finally being arrested. The joking words of a retired military friend of my father's kept creeping into my head. "Yoel," he had said one evening over kebabs at an Arab restaurant in Abu Gosh, "we sure could use you in weapons procurement in New York. Think of how nice it would be. You wouldn't have to leave America, and you'd still get to serve the state." I shuddered and broke into a cold sweat.

At that point, my seatmate turned to me and introduced herself. Her name was Elika and she was traveling from Rotterdam to work on a kibbutz. "They're one of the last socialist communities left in the world," she explained. "I thought I'd get my chance before they disappear altogether."

"That's probably a good idea," I muttered rather cynically, expecting her to be shocked at all of the high-tech industrial work being carried out on kibbutzim these days. Not eager to carry on the conversation with this starry-eyed, hippie-looking young leftist seeking salvation in agrarian neo-socialism, I fell back asleep. I awoke as I felt the wheels of the plane touching the ground.

Bleary-eyed from my eighteen-hour journey, I looked out at the airport tarmac and saw several rows of camouflage Israeli C-130 Hercules transport planes parked in the distance. I slowly stumbled along, laptop in hand, thinking that I needed to check my email and get another cup of coffee. We boarded a bus that drove us to the immigration area, where all of the Palestinian women I'd been traveling with cut in front of me. Determined to be a nice liberal guy, I posed no objections, only to find myself stuck in the slowest line. No one gets singled out more quickly for special attention from the authorities than a Palestinian in an Israeli airport.

An hour and a half later, it was my turn. The immigration officers giggled when they asked for my Israeli passport and I told them that I didn't have one. They insisted on speaking to me in Hebrew. I finally relented. It felt good. Employing that tongue was weirdly reassuring, despite the fact that my Hebrew has suffered greatly. One officer smiled, handed me my papers, and said in a sweet and endearing voice, "*Litraod, Yoel.*"

Carrying my bags into the waiting area, I expected to hear my father whistling to me from within the huge crowd of pale Jewish people whose heavy Slavic accents suggested they were mostly recent immigrants. But my dad wasn't there. I started to worry that he had forgotten to pick me up.

I put my bags down. Finally, someone yelled out, "*Shalom, Yoel!*" It was Dad's friend Israel, sent to pick me up. We had a long drive ahead of us. On the way to Caesarea, we passed Bar-Ilan University, stereotyped by Western news media as a breeding ground for religious nationalists like Yigal Amir, the assassin of former Prime Minister Yitzhak Rabin. It's really weird coming home, I mused. The country always looks busier. Everything is always new. The cars are all shiny, the soldiers have more powerful guns. The highways are lined with American stores. Actually, this time around, Israel looked a lot like Los Angeles to me.

"Who can complain?" Israel asked on the drive, as he pointed to an Office Depot/Toys R Us/Ace Hardware shopping complex to our left. "Under socialism, we only had the necessary items, and even then they were constantly in short supply. Now, everything is easier, though it appears that Netanyahu will ruin it for us again."

"Y'all elected him," I answered. "The people should have known better."

We stopped at a small petrol station on the coastal highway between Ramat Ha Sharon and Netanya. A young Sephardi attendant in blue coveralls, with pierced ears, 1960s GI-issue black plastic frame indie-rock-dork glasses, and a thick black ponytail immediately filled the tank. We got back on the highway without paying for the gas. "Why didn't you give him any money?" I asked.

Israel smiled. "It's a new system we have here where you can have your petrol purchases immediately debited from your bank account through your license-plate number," he responded. "It's a modern country now, Yoel. Things have changed a lot since you lived here."

We eventually departed the highway and pulled up to my father's house. Large brick walls surround the house he designed and built for himself, having achieved affluence in his old age. Telephones were ringing, faxes coming in, beepers going off. Spanish, Hebrew, English, and German could be heard in the distance. My tall, formerly blond-haired-and-blue-eyed seventy-eight-year-old father emerged from his office and gave me his characteristic he-man hug. My frame shuddered with pain. My father's face beamed. "Welcome home, child."

I drank some espresso and sat down to scan the English-language edition of *Ha'aretz*. Five soldiers had been critically wounded in southern Lebanon in an ambush by Iranian-backed Hezbollah guerillas. A remote-controlled bomb had blown up while they were on a routine patrol within Israel's thirty-kilometer security zone in southern Lebanon. The newspaper listed their names, ranks, hometowns, and ages. None were over twenty-two.

Next to that story was a piece on how the Israeli economy had deteriorated since Netanyahu took power two years earlier.

The unemployment rate was hovering near thirteen percent. Welfare services were being cut. The salaries of civil servants were frozen, despite a large increase in the cost of living. In order to slash the deficit, government-run businesses were being sold off to foreign investors. "It's just like America," remarked one commentator.

Underneath this story was an article on the forthcoming Gay Pride Day, the first one ever in Israel. The religious authorities were, of course, condemning it. Israel's transsexual disco superstar, Dana International, was scheduled to sing her hit "Diva" on a parade float as the day's highlight. I stared at a picture of Dana in all her transgressive, dangerously erotic glory. *What a big middle finger to the establishment*, I thought to myself. *It's so punk rock. God, it's good to be back home.*

Feeling a little overwhelmed by it all, I went out on the porch and gazed at the early night sky. Several Apache attack helicopters were flying south in formation over a golf course, probably returning from a retaliatory raid. I turned around and walked back inside. I was tired.

"Time to eat, junior!" bellowed my dad in his pretend 1950s *Leave-it-to-Beaver* English. "We're going to a place where they serve your favorite food." Some of my best memories from my childhood were trips to restaurants in the Palestinian town of Ramallah. But it was now impossible to drive there because Ramallah resided within one of the areas governed by the Palestinian Authority. We would go to an Israeli restaurant that served the same Arab dishes instead.

We drove down a narrow, badly paved road through a field. My father's truck bumped and heaved. Small, dilapidated houses with red-tiled roofs lined the street. This was the Israel I knew as a child. Dusty, old, semi-rural. I was in for a shock. We suddenly entered an American-style shopping plaza. In front of us stood a

McDonald's. To our right was an Ace Hardware, overweight Hasidic men with Brooklyn accents streaming out the front door. On our left was the destination, the 206 Restaurant, which, given the American flavor of everything in this commercial area, was presumably named after Seattle's area code.

As we parked the car, several Arab women wearing *chadors* and carrying McDonald's bags walked by. "Where are we?" I asked.

"A kibbutz," my father replied.

Stunned, I gasped, "You must be joking!"

"No, Yoel," my father said. "Israel's catching up to Europe. Even the old kibbutznik Reds are embracing market socialism. Everything here is collectively owned, even the American fast-food restaurant."

I thought back to Elika, the Dutch woman I had met on the airplane. I wondered if her pursuit of "one of the last socialist communities" had her working at a collectively owned McDonald's. It was too much. I wanted to throw up.

The next day flew by in a chaotic frenzy. Visiting a new shopping mall with my stepmother Ana in the neighboring town of Ofakim, where Babushka-wearing Russian women strolled through the supermarket carrying shopping carts full of Wonder Bread, beets, and imported Birds Eye frozen peas, I felt like the foreigner that Israelis perceived me to be. A great deal had changed. There was so much affluence, so much culture, so many things American, and yet, so little peace of mind. I took leave of Ana for a moment and wandered the aisles in a jetlagged daze, thinking about diva Dana International and helicopter gunships flying over golf courses, recalling the daily casualty reports in the newspaper. As I picked up a quarter-pound bag of Lavazza espresso imported from Italy, I realized that I had been yearning to re-experience the sentimental pleasantries of a Labor Zionist childhood. Instead, I was getting a shock treatment in the brutal lessons of post–Cold War global capitalism.

When we got home, my father—never one to leave his military background completely behind—handed me my itinerary. I was to go pick up my brother David and his family at the airport. Then I was supposed to drive them to Jerusalem, where we were to meet at a new Moroccan restaurant called Darna, just off of Jaffa Street, the main drag.

I hopped into Elie's Korean-made truck and embarked on the two-hour journey in rush-hour traffic. While merging onto the highway, I turned on Reshet Gimmel, the popular music subdivision of Israel's public radio network, Kol Yisrael. The disc jockey was playing a song from the latest album by American "post-rockers" Tortoise, followed by retro lounge act Combustible Edison, hip-hopper Wyclef Jean, and Nusrat Fateh Ali Khan, the great Qawali singer from Pakistan. I laughed. Tortoise, an Israeli favorite! Who woulda thunk? It sure beat the hell out of the requisite and inescapable old patriotic sing-alongs from my childhood, like the '67 victory anthem, *"Yerushalayim Shel Zahav"* ("Jerusalem the Golden"). My amusement was enough to keep my spirits up all the way to the airport. Now that's what I call World Beat.

When I arrived at Ben Gurion airport, my brother David was already emerging from immigration. He looked very tired, but happy to see me. "Gimme a cigarette," he barked. We smoked together in silence, scanning the newly arrived: excited Christian tourists looking for their television-minister guides; Jewish-American teenagers on Zionist youth summer vacations; fat Greek Orthodox patriarchs just off the plane from Athens; blond, long-haired German Jesus-freaks lugging huge internal-frame packs. "So, this is what the great Zionist founders envisioned for the Holy Land?" David remarked. "They built a country so that pilgrims could go sightseeing in freedom. What a joke."

As we drove up the new highway to Jerusalem, David surveyed

the landscape. "Look at that goddamned sprawl. It's all so thoughtless," he said. "Israelis seem to put up buildings anywhere they want, without regard for the landscape, without lip service to any aesthetics or artistry that would incorporate the architecture into the scenery tastefully. They don't have any concept of zoning laws. It's gross. This all used to be beautiful farmland, and now look at it. Cheaply constructed industrial parks with neon billboards. It looks like southern California."

"I know," I said, laughing somberly. "In their haste to create a country, they indiscriminately build on top of anything, anywhere there is an iota of construction space to be found. The irony is that these are the fields where the army fought the Jordanians during the War of Independence." We drove for a while in silence.

Fifty years ago, the new Jewish army, full of untrained conscripts and death-camp survivors, had fought Jordan's mighty Arab Legion and scores of armed Palestinian militiamen from local villages to maintain access to the city. Entering the forested Judean foothills to begin our ascent to the city, we could see the rusted wreckage of armored supply trucks destroyed by opposing forces that still littered the side of the highway. They constituted the remains of convoys that our father, among many others, had helped organize to supply the Jewish half of Jerusalem in 1948.

Every time we drove to Jerusalem when we were kids, Elie reminded us of this fact. It invariably turned what was supposed to be a joyous, fun trip to an exotic, ancient city into a tour of a roadside mausoleum. We resented Elie for it, as the stories ceased to have any significance in their repetition. At a certain point, I felt that his nostalgia was an excuse rather than a reminder, but I didn't know what the excuse was for, and I was too young to figure it out.

We were snapped back into the present as we entered the outskirts of Jerusalem, in awe of all the new high-rises and housing complexes made of orange Jerusalem stone jutting into the twilight sky to the north. This was Jerusalem's new periphery, well-known for its American immigrants—some orthodox, some religious nationalists, but mostly ultra-orthodox Hasids, as Americans tend to identify them (Haredim, or "Trembling Ones," as they are called in Hebrew). At a time when Israel was governed by a democratically elected right-wing demagogue espousing the merciless anti-welfare-state ideology of Reagan, Thatcher, Gingrich, Clinton, and Blair, the main recipients of government handouts and public-housing subsidies were these highly reactionary communities of Jews inhabiting the hills surrounding the edges of the city.

While the views of nationalist religious Jews are repugnant to many mainstream Israelis, the contempt with which they hold them pales in comparison to the derogatory attitudes that most Israelis take toward the Haredi community. Until the Al-Aksa Intifada brought the problematic nature of the Israeli settlements in the Occupied Territories back into painful focus—in particular, the nationalist religious ideologies that justify holding onto the land—the Haredim bore the brunt of most liberal Israeli scorn. Why? Because the Haredi community aspires to a peculiar kind of spiritual aristocracy through their reliance on public funding for a combination of religious study and partisan political advocacy.

Exempt from compulsory military service, but extremely aggressive when it comes to demanding a voice in government policy, the Haredim draw a lot of fire for being unwilling to do the dirty work of defending the nation and creating wealth. And they bring this on, to a certain extent, by demonstrating a distinct lack of mercy in their treatment of other Jews. For example, Haredi religious authorities insist that immigrants who cannot demonstrate that they were born of a Jewish mother be ineligible for Israeli citizenship. When Tel Aviv's Dolphinarium

Discotheque was bombed in June 2001, killing twenty-one mostly teenage Russian immigrants, the Haredi-controlled state burial society initially refused several of the victims interment rights in public cemeteries because their Jewish heritage was "subject to debate." As my father said later, "What these American fundamentalists really want is to turn Israel into a modern-day Jewish Iran."

After an uneventful dinner in Jerusalem, we checked into our hotel. My room was on the sixth floor, overlooking the city. I lit a cigarette, strolled onto the balcony in the pitch-black night, and gazed out at the Old City. I was so tired I could barely think, but I found the soft wind on my sweaty body soothing. I began to consider that what I fear most may not be the New Jerusalem sought by fundamentalist Christians but the one being built by fundamentalist Jews. As scary as Christianity can be for someone with my background, I can still keep it at arm's length. More upsetting is the realization that I have something in common with the Israeli and American Jews who would be truly content with a Jewish Iran. My heart raced as I weighed this prospect. I took one last look at the sleeping holy city and turned off the lights. I knew now why I'd come here.

It seemed like the phone had been ringing forever. When I finally lifted the receiver, I could hear my father's voice: "Get down here immediately, child, we have a Bat Mitzvah to go to." Frustrated that I hadn't had a chance to drink any coffee, I got dressed and made a mad dash for the elevator.

"So, you finally got your ass out of bed, chief," said David, as I stepped into the lobby. "Let's get out of here."

My older brother knows Jerusalem well, and he navigated us to the entrance of the Old City in minutes. We parked and began walking in the already hot early-morning sunlight to the Damascus Gate. Border troops with their trademark bright-green berets and collapsing-butt M-16s were glancing around, chattering incessantly on walkie-talkies, fingers resting uneasily on their triggers. We marched down dusty stone steps toward a lush, green garden hidden underneath the *Migdal David* (Tower of David).

After a little while, the ceremony began. A conservative rabbi from the Hebrew University commenced speaking in a thick Brooklyn accent. He looked like a typical Baby Boomer who had rediscovered his Jewish roots and decided to immigrate. The rabbi spoke about the concept of maturity, and how God views it. Then he introduced my niece Odíle, and together they started reading the Torah.

Odíle's voice was a little shaky. She read in English. The rabbi answered her in Hebrew in call-and-response pattern much like a rap song, breaking into prayer every now and then in a lilting New-York-cum-Eastern-European cadence that raised the hair on the back of my neck. Fifteen minutes later, the rabbi issued authoritative platitudes about assuming the responsibilities of an adult according to Jewish law. I began to nod out. Suddenly, the ceremony was over. I was overwhelmed with relief. But everyone sat in silence. My father took over.

"It gives me such great pleasure to see my family here today," he started. "Nothing makes me happier than to have my children here in Israel to celebrate my oldest grandchild's birthday. Especially at such a crucial time in Jewish history as this, when the nation is again dividing itself up into two halves, the pure and the statists, much like in the Old Testament when the children of Israel divided themselves up into two nations: the nation of Israel and the nation of Judah.

"I want to remind you all that this is a repetition of something that happened long ago, and that we must view it in such perspective if we are going to overcome the unjust divisions which my generation was never able to foresee happening again. If we do this, we'll have the resources and the knowledge to know that one day we'll be far beyond this cruel repeat of history, which can only be read as a symptom of the suffering of a long persecuted people unequipped to deal with having built a nation for the first time in two thousand years of tragic history."

As my father left the podium, we all remained silent. Static sounded from the walkie-talkies carried by the soldiers, white noise bouncing like bursts of automatic gunfire off of the walls of the ancient city which surrounded us. The memories radiating from these archaic slabs of stone mingled with the echo of my father's stern words, set off by the footsteps of clueless Christian tourists being herded up the steps of the Tower of David by Palestinian tour guides. Out of the corner of my eye, I caught one of the tourists staring down at me and wondered what he was thinking. Embarrassed, he turned away.

Finally, the rabbi had us stand and recite a closing prayer. "*Baruch Ata-Adonai*," everyone sang, "*Eleunu Melech Ha Olam*." Tears had started to well up in my eyes. Feeling self-conscious, I wiped them on my sleeve so that nobody would see. I thought to myself that the significance of this trip wasn't so much recognizing my niece's coming of age as it was recognizing my entire family's entrance into something resembling political maturity. Not only as a distinct group of people biologically related to each other, but as the microcosm of a new nation that my father had unfortunately raised us to be.

For the first time since I was a child, I was filled with a naïve hope—the kind that's inspired by watching people learn from their mistakes, knowing that they'll be able to move beyond them. Enough history and enough tragedy had transpired to force us all to cut through the bullshit ideologies that shelter a family—or a country—from the truth of its existence. For now, at least, we were no longer in denial. "All this shit will surely pass," I mumbled under my breath as we left the Old City. "Netanyahu, the killing, the history, the segregation, the religion. Everything."

❖

It would be nice to end this story—and this book—with this moment of reconciliation. But it would mean compromising the realization that made it special. Life goes on, progress may not. Right now, it's hard to sustain any sense of optimism where Israel is concerned. Instead of moving toward peace, today's participants in the conflict have turned back to the perverse security of a state of war. For my family, thankfully, the outlook is brighter. Yet even there, the contentment of our reunion in Jerusalem has given way to the complexities of a life weighed down with the burden of history. So, while I continue to treasure my memories of that hopeful moment, I will not sacrifice the reality that made it so meaningful. Instead, I'll move both back in time and closer to the present, as a way of confronting the latest resurgence of hard-line politics in the divided land my father described.

Not long after the beginning of the Al-Aksa Intifada in late-September 2000, I traveled to Israel with my new girlfriend, Courtney, to hear my father give a speech honoring my pioneering great-grandfather, Eleazar Elhanan Schalit. It was the opening of a museum on the site of Eleazar's restored home, "*Bet Schalit*" ("Schalit House"), located in *Kikar H'Meyaodim* ("Founder's Square") in Rishon Le Zion. The city had been catapulted into notoriety for the Rishon Symphony's taboo-breaking performance of Wagner's *Siegfried Idyll* and *Till Eulenspiegel*, along with a work by Richard Strauss, a similarly anti-Semitic German composer, during a noontime concert several days before the museum's inauguration. This formerly agricultural settlement of just over 200,000 inhabitants had been founded under the patronage of Zionist philanthropist Baron Edmund de Rothschild through the efforts of seventeen families, including my own.

Sitting in the front row of the auditorium listening to Elie, I was overcome with shame when he stated that he would paraphrase his talk in English for the non-Hebrew speakers in the audience. I expressed my discomfort at my linguistic shortcomings by repositioning my legs once again, quietly berating myself. *I'll miss the real gist of his talk*, I thought. *Dad's getting so old, he'll probably say something entirely different when he attempts to translate himself, and I'll forever be kicking myself for purposely forgetting my second tongue.*

It's not as though my father says things in public that he doesn't also disclose in private. Regardless of his aging process, he remains effortlessly consistent. No matter what I'd miss that night, I knew I'd be able to get it out of him later. The point was his timing. With a two-and-a-half-week-old war being fought less than twenty miles away in the West Bank, the Gaza Strip, and Jerusalem, I knew my father would not miss this opportunity to remind the audience that his country was still far from being complete, that normalization without peace is neither normal, nor legitimate. I wanted to bathe in the immediacy of his words.

Instead, all I heard was myself, and the echoes of my own feelings of estrangement from the language of my father and the culture he'd chosen to transmit. Every once in a while, I'd get pulled out of my thoughts by Hebrew terms that I associate with violence, such as *milhama* (war), when they'd roll off my father's tongue. But otherwise, I felt myself lost in the velocity of where Elie's language was leading me, specifically to the heartbreaking disappointment and shame I'd first experienced after the murder of eight hundred Palestinians in Beirut's Sabra and Shatila refugee camps in 1982 (some estimates put the death toll as high as 1500). With our military's consent, Lebanese Christian militiamen had entered these centers and spent two nights wantonly killing civilians.

The military official responsible for this massacre—former Minister of Defense Ariel Sharon, founder of Israel's right-wing Likud party and, as I write this in September of 2001, Israel's current prime minister—was the same man whose September 28, 2000 visit to Jerusalem's Al-Aksa Mosque sparked the fighting being waged during my visit. Comparing the Israel Defense Force's culpability in the Beirut massacre to that of Russian and Polish authorities for anti-Semitic pogroms in the nineteenth century, a government-appointed commission found in February 1983 that Sharon and the Israeli military were "indirectly responsible" for the slaughter; Sharon, however, was never officially charged. But the blood his leadership permitted to be shed stained more than the reputation of Israel's vaunted army. It also had profound political implications for a whole generation of Jews, both Israeli and American, who found themselves reassessing their relationship with Israel. The brutality problematized one of the chief mythologies about Israel and the Jewish people—that two thousand years of persecution, topped off by the Holocaust, had turned us into the most morally self-reflexive of people. Lebanon was our first national theodicy.

As I have said, I was one of those disenchanted people, the son of a second-generation Israeli family that had arrived from Riga via the Ukraine in 1882, toward the end of the Ottoman Empire's rule of Palestine. Even though we were one of the steepest and most orthodox of secular Zionist families, the Sabra and Shatila killings threw us into an intense crisis that called into question the moral justification of our entire political orientation. My older sister Naomi and I were shattered by these events. We were not only forced to reexamine our family's politics; we were also forced to physically separate ourselves from Israel.

In order to understand what a traumatic experience this was

for us, it is important to grasp the metaphorical meaning that Israel held for several generations of Jews: Israel was not just the country that we shared as a place of historical origin; it was also Zion, a religiously inspired ideal of perfect justice that Europe, with its centuries of anti-Semitism and death, could not offer us. We were never anything but refugees. By returning to "the promised land," the only country according to the Bible (and racist Europeans) in which we ever belonged, my family attempted to transform two thousand years of collective frustration and despair into something positive, something emancipatory, hoping for a sense of stability that we'd historically been denied.

To the extent that my family considers ourselves "Israelis," this label betrays the anachronistic legacy of an identity formed in transnational exile and then transported back to the Middle East. There, being "Israeli" suggested a whole new set of meanings that we did not actually share with our friends and family in Caesarea, Haifa, and Tel Aviv, regardless of whether or not we spoke the same language. This was not always the case.

The nineteenth-century revival of the Hebrew language, not just for prayer, but for everyday life, was a way of distilling all of these hopes and aspirations into a common political discourse which would open up a new way of being ourselves. Thus, one can imagine why here, at the opening of a museum dedicated to my great-grandfather's achievements in helping found the city of Rishon Le Zion (First of Zion), the very first Palestinian Jewish municipality after the Jewish people were originally expelled from the region by the Romans at the beginning of the first millennium, I was feeling a little guilty. How could I not? This town was literally *made* for me, and here I was, the great-grandson of one of its architects, unable to comprehend the native tongue.

When I was growing up—a native English speaker in a quadrilingual household—Hebrew always carried an air of moral significance and hysterical urgency, even if it was invoked in reference to the mundane. Every time we spoke the language, it was like we were reinventing the world. Hebrew wasn't merely the language of a new colonialism brought by white refugees from Europe; it was also a language of survival, burdened with the memories of a former national community that had been driven into exile by European imperialism two centuries earlier.

Hebrew assumed a new meaning for my father's generation. Even as it retained the burden of our history, it was imbued with the promise of the new Israel. Hebrew was the language of a brand new country that their generation had established. Using it so effortlessly, so fluently, they demonstrated their own cultural commitment to building this nation, particularly in the shadow of the Holocaust to which they bore personal witness. Because they lived in Palestine, they had survived when so many others perished. Yet World War II touched them no less deeply. My father, a citizen of the British Commonwealth, served as a maritime patrol-plane navigator for the Royal Canadian Air Force, first in Canada's Maritime Provinces and later in Europe. My then-teenage mother lost her first husband to a US Air Force plane crash, from which she never emotionally recovered.

The ghosts of these events hovered in the background as I listened to my father finish his speech. I took in Elie's syllables carefully, keeping them fresh in my ears, waiting to hear other fragments of these histories in the accent of the speaker who would follow him, maybe Russian, maybe Arabic. But I heard none: The next speaker was pure Israeli, disconnected from the mid-century past of my parents' generation. There was no sense of the complexity I had detected in my father's voice. I sat through the rest of this gentleman's address feeling an emptiness; I could not hear anything other than the unacceptable present in his voice. I was able to comprehend most of what he was saying: He was thanking the donors who helped fund the museum of which this auditorium was a part, making sure to note how such institutions are important reminders of where the state of Israel started, and why we need to be grateful to those who help subsidize such monuments. You know, the same old fundraiser's gratitude story.

While I had expected such a talk, I couldn't get comfortable with how often he invoked my family's last name. Perhaps I couldn't completely accept that the event was a dedication to my pioneering great-grandfather. Perhaps the constant invocation of our name depersonalized it, while the violent present obscured the nation-building achievements for which it was being credited.

Then it came to me. I felt like a fraud because I'd forced myself to lose my Hebrew out of rebellion against my family, out of disgust with the moral inconsistencies of Israel. By choosing to forget the language with which our country was forged, I had disavowed my family's legacy in the founding of the nation. I was symbolically disqualified from participating in the evening's event.

I felt bad for my father. This was his night, his victory, yet I could not come to terms with our family's political legacy. What I really wanted was an acknowledgment of what we had *not* achieved as a family. Our experience of oppression in Europe should have driven us to realize genuinely inclusive multicultural political ideals. But today's Israel is even worse at accommodating ethnic and religious difference than the United States.

I tried to ease my discomfort by subjecting each subsequent speaker to a peculiar linguistic scrutiny, listening for traces of the nineteenth century, of immigration, of incompleteness in the way they spoke Hebrew. I wanted confirmation that my inability to remain fluent was a means of expressing our failure to follow through on our national project. Somehow, if there were remnants of the outside world, of badly conjugated verbs redolent of other languages still present in our national discourse, there would be a sense that our work in creating a just society was far from being done. And this, in turn, would mean that there was still hope for progress.

After the speeches were over, I walked outside with my girlfriend to get some coffee. We took our drinks with us and stared up at my great-grandfather's restored home while my father walked up the steps, followed by a line of Hasidic cousins whom I had absolutely no interest in meeting. A loud, sustained wail took me by surprise. The Hasidim had started singing in a deep, Eastern-European brogue that could have been the voices of a congregation in a Warsaw synagogue two hundred years ago. I couldn't believe it. Elie, in all his anti-clerical graciousness, was letting these religious relatives bless his resolutely anti-Hasidic (*mitnaged* in Hebrew) grandfather's house. *What prayer are these creatures singing?* I wondered. Once again, I found myself confounded by a lack of understanding. Not only could I not comprehend their Hebrew, I couldn't even identify the specific prayer.

I sipped my coffee and laughed. At least I could grasp the ritual well enough to make sense of what these people were actually doing. But, as usual, it was an understanding mediated by a framework born of my own past—as a former Israeli who was willing to forsake his citizenship out of protest, and as a secular Jew who only understood the meaning of religious rituals contextually. I couldn't help but experience the irony of my linguistic displacement. It was as if I inhabited a uniquely alienated space between eternal exile and national reconquest. Was I fortunate or simply fucked? Could my inability to speak the language really be a way of recapturing the original utopian spirit of Zionism, before it was drenched in the blood of state-making? I thought of the wax figures of nineteenth-century Jewish settlers inside the museum reconstruction of my great-grandfather's home. I imagined them listening to the blessing that was being bestowed upon their new household. What would they make of these pasty retro-medievalists, with their cellphones and their wig-wearing wives? *It's a good thing we don't speak the same language*, I told myself. *These Hasids' tongues raise inanimate objects to life. Mine leaves the dead alone.* I knew my thoughts were cruel, but I couldn't help myself.

Ultra-orthodox Jews conceal their racist ideology of an ethnically pure Jewish polity in their spirituality, while simultaneously attacking the legitimacy of the secular Zionist state. There will be no justifiable Jewish existence, they reason, until the coming of the *Moshiach*, the messiah. These "holy" people let non-religious Jews do the dirty work of keeping the Arabs down, sacrificing their children to the army, while they await the *real* Israel. It's a contradiction that portends as violent and divisive a conflict between secular and religious Israelis as the present one between Muslims and Jews. But until the conclusion of a real peace agreement between Palestine and Israel, such a clash of Jewish cultures will be permanently postponed. If there is any value that the Israeli side accrues by the perpetuation of war with the Arab states, this is it. I could feel the seeds of the coming conflict in my own ambivalence toward the religious members of my family as they sanctified our ancestral home. How could these people be sanctifying anything at the current historical moment?

To bless my great-grandfather's home was to sanctify the destructive status quo currently overtaking our country. No such liberties would be permitted in my ideal world until long after the guns stopped firing, the rocks stopped being thrown, and the suicide bombers ceased detonating themselves in our shopping malls and our open-air markets. I knew I should be more forgiving, because in my heart of Marxist hearts I could see that my family's religiosity was no less a product of the stress of historical circumstance than my own confusion, even if they had chosen to *believe* instead of think. I also knew that rendering this judgment on my own flesh and blood was highly patronizing. When one of my Hasidic cousins came up and introduced himself and his family, I forced myself to relax and shake his hand, replying in an easy Hebrew that I couldn't believe I was using. *"Naim Meod"* ("Nice to meet you"), I warmly replied. *"Ani Yoel, ha ben shel Elie"* ("I'm Joel, the son of Elie"). Maybe it was because the guy seemed perfectly harmless and a little personal interaction was all it would take to overcome my deep-seated animosity.

As Courtney and I drove home later that evening, we turned on the radio. Moving through the stations, the only thing we could pick up were modern-rock programs, Pearl Jam and Radiohead blasting out of nearly every frequency of Middle-Eastern airwave space. Not in the mood for rock and roll, and frustrated by our lack of options, we continued scanning the dial until our car pulled up to an intersection where a wooden reproduction of the founder of the Zionist movement, Theodor Herzl, was casting a shadow over the highway from atop a water tower. We could hear an Islamic mullah reciting a Friday night prayer in rapid-fire Arabic at an almost techno-like tempo of 120 beats-per-minute. We both laughed at how much more appropriate it was to be rocked by this Islamic equivalent of rapping than by bad grunge. However, our descent into the pleasures of truly "alternative" local culture was interrupted by the unexpected eruption of its political subtext.

The radio host began turning the mullah on and off, announcing in Arabic between blasts of prayer the names of "occupied" Palestinian cities: Tel Aviv, Haifa, Bat Yam, Netanya—all Jewish communities alleged by this broadcast to be built upon the remains of former Arab ones. The list went on and on, as did the mullah. In that moment, I recognized why I had been able to communicate with my cousin in my long-dormant Hebrew. It was because I understood the basic political structures underlying the "language" that informed this broadcast—the language of the Intifada, of the struggle for liberation from division and violence; a language based on the longing for a conclusion to hatred and death; a language that Jews also know, regardless of how long we've suppressed it.

I'm gonna learn this language one day, I thought, as I fumbled around the car looking for my Minidisc recorder. *But until I do, I'm at least going to make sure I get a good recording of it.*

On the road to Nahariya, Northern Israel, 2000

EPILOGUE

As the cantor began singing *"Shema Israel,"* he turned and faced the Israeli flag hanging from a pole beside the stage. I adjusted my skull-cap on the back of my bald head and stood up rather shakily. Staring at the blue and white Star of David–adorned pennant in front of me, I listened as the mourners in the pews behind us began to follow the cantor's words, and wondered how I would feel if it were an American flag we were all facing.

Recalling an anti-Semitic sermon I once heard on a Christian talk show about how Jews can never be *true* Americans because their religion demands conflicting national loyalties, I chuckled beneath my breath in sarcastic agreement and began to sing along with the congregation. As much as I felt myself overcome by the funereal sadness of the *Shema,* I was grateful for the ironic relief that this unconscious coupling of my brother's fate with my family's national identity had cast upon the proceedings.

While I have sung the *Shema* on numerous occasions over the course of my life, I find it hard not to separate the prayer from the event at which I was first taught it as a child: on Holocaust

Memorial Day, in Israel. No matter where I am, every time I hear it being recited, the deep, droning swells evoke a profound sadness for the millions of European Jews who perished during the Second World War, more than a small number of whom were members of my own family. There are very few songs, religious or otherwise, that reconcile the personal and the political for me like this prayer.

It's not just a song to end all songs, so to speak. To paraphrase a statement Theodor Adorno made in the late 1960s, one cannot write poetry after Auschwitz. Because I was raised to associate this piece of liturgical solemnity with commemorating a catastrophe that resists any kind of objectification, it has always demanded the most painful of silences following its utterance.

In the final weeks of completing this book, this day was going to prove an exception to that dramatic rule. As the congregation broke into the song's coda—*"Adonai Eluenu, Adonai Echad"*—I could hear the voice of my brother speaking into my answering machine the week before.

"Nu shmendrick," his voice stuttered in Yiddish, "is everything okay? I'm just about to drive the kids up to summer camp in North Carolina, and I wanted to make sure that you had my cellphone number in case you needed me."

Shit, I thought as the *Shema* ended, *that was the last time I will ever hear him.*

All of a sudden, the ceremony was over. My brother's voice tapered off into the sounds of static from his mobile phone, which, as usual, he had difficulty hanging up. The cantor had stopped singing and was announcing that my sister-in-law would be hosting a reception on behalf of our family immediately afterwards. Following Nina and her three children with my remaining siblings, we quietly walked out the door and onto the steps of the synagogue where mourners had gathered to pay their respects to my family and express their regrets.

My third trip to a synagogue since the late 1970s, I was ritually observing the death of my second oldest brother in Miami, a city that had once been described to me as "the anti-Jerusalem, the place that old New York Jews go to die." Although the only thing I really wanted was to get carried home on a stretcher, there were mourners I still had to attend to, like the extremely old woman in front of me who had been standing there for quite a while, trying to get my attention.

"Are you going to bring your brother's body back home to Israel?" she burst out in a shrill New-York-meets-Warsaw accent.

"No," I replied rather softly. "Michael requested that we cremate him and spread his ashes over his favorite fishing ground at sea."

"Baruch ha-shem" ("Bless his name"), the old lady said to me, flashing a forearm with a fading tattoo of numbers on it. "I wish you and your family well."

Michael Aryeh, I thought as she stiffly walked away, *you may have had the misfortune to die in Miami, but your ashes will find the home of their own choosing.*

As my siblings and I piled into our rental car and attempted to drive to the reception that followed, we got lost in the seemingly endless maze of dead-end streets and multiple repeats of similarly numbered suburban roads that circle the gated community that Michael and his family called home.

How on earth could anyone know where their home is in a town like this? I kept thinking, as my brother David called friends and family members trying to figure out how to get to the reception. *No wonder they need to feel like they belong somewhere else. Miami is about more than dying. It's also about not knowing how the hell to find your fucking family.*

"We just passed three separate 122nd Avenues," I could hear David telling Michael's secretary on his cellphone. "Which is the right one to take a left on?" She didn't know.

Hanging up his mobile in exasperation, David decided to stop at a gas station and ask for directions. Even though my brother's home turned out to be less than half a mile away, the attendants had no idea how to guide us.

"Maybe we weren't meant to get there," my sister Naomi intoned, as we sped off, directionless, and passed a new housing development.

Laughing, David cynically replied, "What do you mean? This place looks so much like a jazzed-up Tel Aviv, it's hard to imagine we were ever lost."

Also from Akashic Books

We Own You Nothing: Punk Planet, the Collected Interviews
Edited by Daniel Sinker
334 pages, paperback (6" x 9"), ISBN: 1-888451-14-9
Price: $16.95

"This collection of interviews reflects one of *Punk Planet's* most important qualities: Sinker's willingness to look beyond the small world of punk bands and labels and deal with larger issues. With interview subjects ranging from punk icons Thurston Moore and Ian MacKaye to Noam Chomsky and representatives of the Central Ohio Abortion Access Fund, as well as many other artists, musicians, and activists, this book is not solely for the tattooed, pierced teenage set. All of the interviews are probing and well thought out, the questions going deeper than most magazines would ever dare; and each has a succinct, informative introduction for readers who are unfamiliar with the subject. Required reading for all music fans." *—Library Journal*

Falun Gong's Challenge to China: Spiritual Practice or "Evil Cult"?
A report and reader by Danny Schechter
288 pages, trade paperback
ISBN: 1-888451-27-0
Price: $15.95

The only book-length investigative report on this severe human rights crisis that is affecting the lives of millions.

"[Schechter] offers a persuasive analysis of this strange and still unfolding story . . ." *—New York Times*

The Big Mango by Norman Kelley
270 pages, trade paperback
ISBN: 1-888451-10-8
Price: $14.95

She's Back! Nina Halligan, Private Investigator.

"Want a scathing social and political satire? Look no further than Kelley's second effort featuring 'bad girl' African-American PI and part-time intellectual Nina Halligan—it's X-rated, but a romp of a read . . . Nina's acid takes on recognizable public figures and institutions both amuse and offend . . . Kelley spares no one, blacks and whites alike, and this provocative novel is sure to attract attention . . ." *—Publishers Weekly*

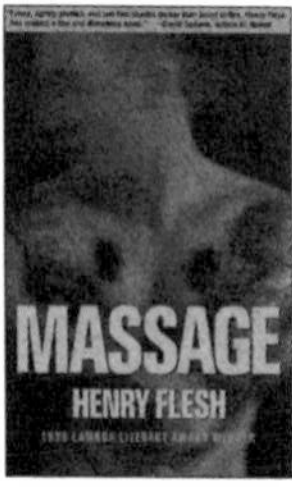

Massage by Henry Flesh
(1999 Lambda Literary Award Winner)
384 pages, trade paperback
ISBN: 1-888451-06-8
Price: $15.95

"Funny, tightly plotted, and just two shades darker than burnt coffee. Henry Flesh has crafted a fine and disturbing novel."
—David Sedaris, author of *Naked*

Heart of the Old Country by Tim McLoughlin
216 pages, trade paperback
ISBN: 1-888451-15-7
Price: $14.95

"Set in a crummy corner of present-day Bay Ridge, Brooklyn, this sweet, sardonic and by turns hilarious and tragic first novel opens with a no-hoper named Michael going through his motions . . . The novel's greatest achievement is its tender depiction of Michael as a would-be tough guy, trying to follow his father's dictum of 'Give them nothing,' while undergoing a painful education in the real world." *—Publishers Weekly*

Adios Muchachos by Daniel Chavarría
245 pages, paperback
ISBN: 1-888451-16-5
Price: $13.95

"Daniel Chavarría has long been recognized as one of Latin America's finest writers. Now he again proves why with *Adios Muchachos,* a comic mystery peopled by a delightfully mad band of miscreants, all of them led by a woman you will not soon forget—Alicia, the loveliest bicycle whore in all Havana."
—Edgar Award-winning author William Heffernan

Water in Darkness by Daniel Buckman
193 pages, hardcover
ISBN: 1-888451-19-X
Price: $21.00

"Simply put, *Water in Darkness* is a superb novel, a tasty piece of storytelling. Daniel Buckman's tale is a roller coaster ride, told from that blunt, dark place where the rubber meets the road. And the writing is gritty, precise, and vivid—like a dream. Here is an earth-bound 'Chicago' style that harkens back to *Studs Lonigan,* and reminds one of the close-to-the-bone, walk-the-plank stories of Mike Royko, Stuart Dybek, and Nelson Algren. Buckman speaks for a new, young generation of soldiers who thought they were at peace. *Water in Darkness* is a sterling piece of work—the best new fiction I have read in a good long while."
—Larry Heinemann, author of *Paco's Story*, winner of the National Book Award

These books are available at local bookstores. They can also be purchased with a credit card online through www.akashicbooks.com. To order by mail send a check or money order to:

Akashic Books
PO Box 1456
New York, NY 10009
www.akashicbooks.com • Akashic7@aol.com

(Prices include shipping. Outside the U.S., add $3 to each book ordered.)

San Francisco, 2000

Joel Schalit is associate editor at Utne Award–winning *Punk Planet Magazine* and co-director of politics and culture journal *Bad Subjects*, the longest running publication on the Internet. He is a contributor to the *San Francisco Bay Guardian*, and is the editor of *The Anti-Capitalism Reader*, forthcoming from Akashic Books. Schalit currently lives and works in San Francisco, where he also serves as a member of the beats and noise agit-prop band *Elders of Zion*.